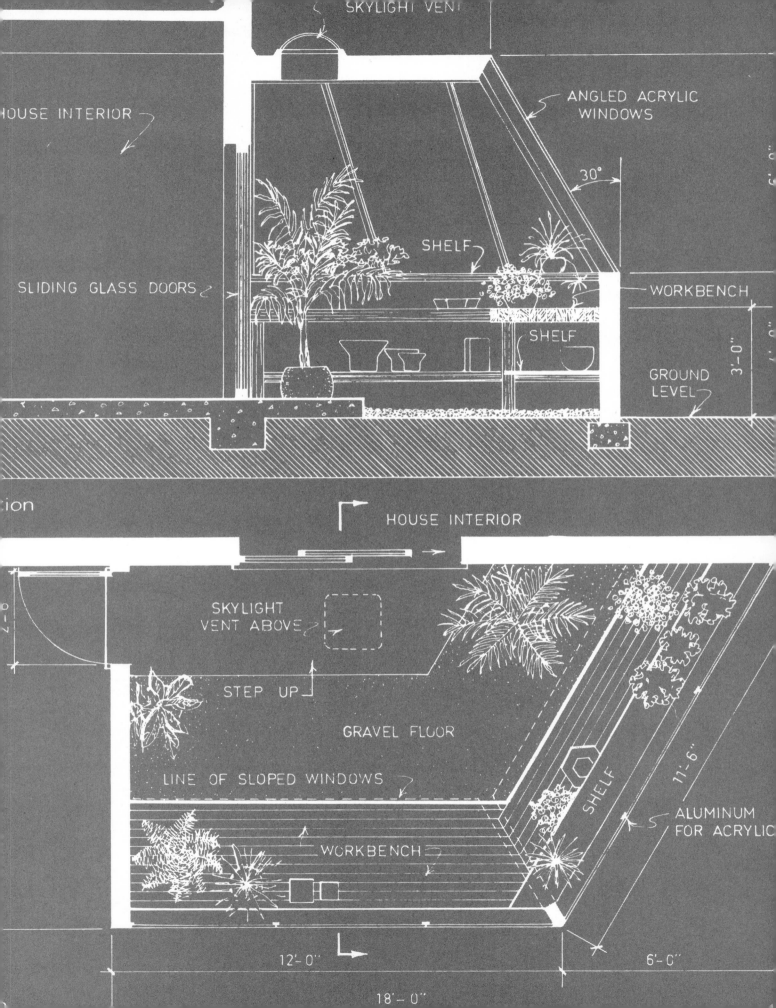

SKYLIGHT VENT

HOUSE INTERIOR

ANGLED ACRYLIC
WINDOWS

30°

SHELF

SLIDING GLASS DOORS

WORKBENCH

SHELF

GROUND
LEVEL

3'-0"

tion

HOUSE INTERIOR

SKYLIGHT
VENT ABOVE

STEP UP

GRAVEL FLOOR

LINE OF SLOPED WINDOWS

SHELF

11'-6"

WORKBENCH

ALUMINUM
FOR ACRYLIC

12'-0"

6'-0"

18'-0"

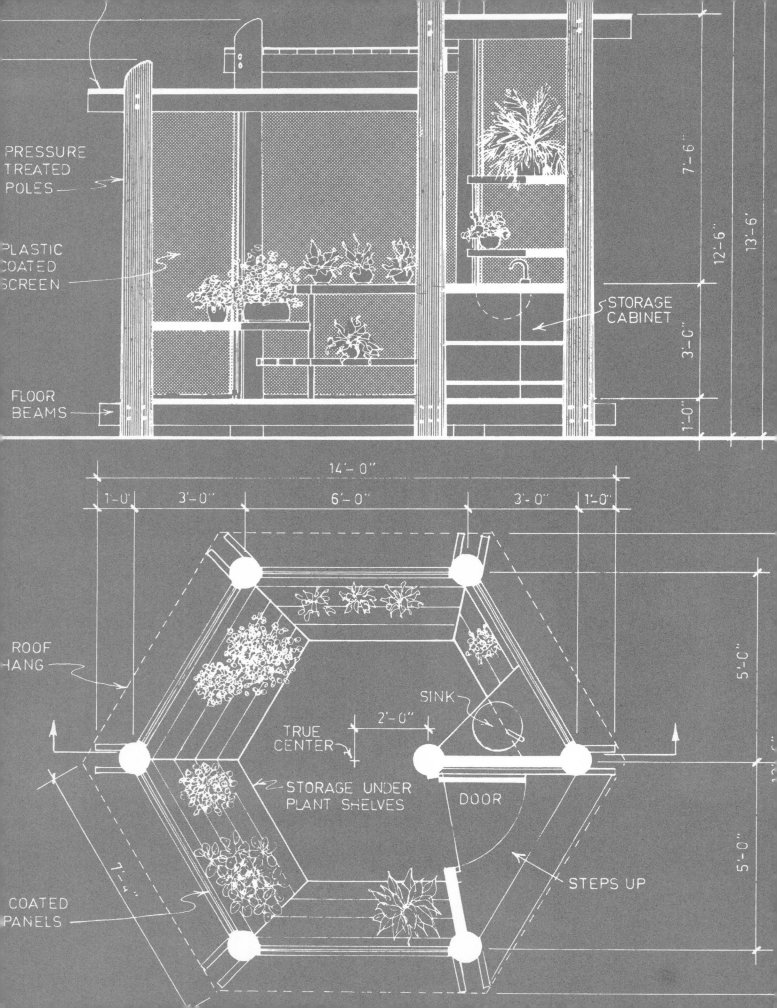

PRESSURE
TREATED
POLES

PLASTIC
COATED
SCREEN

FLOOR
BEAMS

STORAGE
CABINET

7'-6"

12'-6"

13'-6"

3'-0"

1'-0"

14'-0"

1'-0"   3'-0"   6'-0"   3'-0"   1'-0"

ROOF
HANG

SINK

TRUE
CENTER

2'-0"

STORAGE UNDER
PLANT SHELVES

DOOR

STEPS UP

COATED
PANELS

7'-4"

5'-0"

5'-0"

YOUR HOMEMADE GREENHOUSE

and How to Build It

UPDATED & EXPANDED EDITION

JACK KRAMER

CORNERSTONE LIBRARY
New York

Published by Cornerstone Library
A Simon & Schuster Subsidiary of
Gulf & Western Corporation
Simon & Schuster Building
1230 Avenue of the Americas
New York, New York 10020

This new Cornerstone Library edition is published by arrangement with and is a complete and unabridged
reprint of the original hardcover edition

The trademark of Cornerstone Library, Inc. consists of the words "Cornerstone Library" and the portrayal of a
cube and is registered in the United States Patent Office

Manufactured in the United States of America

ISBN 346-12442-5

Acknowledgements

For this book, several greenhouses of many kinds were photographed and I sincerely want to thank the following people for allowing us to photograph their personal places for plants:

Dan Campbell
Don Worth
Ben Botelli
Carol and Red Spediacci
Dan DeGunthen
Hamilton Tyler
Western Springs Nursery

Special gratitude goes to my good friend, Eldon Danhausen, of Chicago, Illinois for photos of his greenhouse, and to the many photographers and artists who worked on this book, my thanks as always.

For reading and making suggestions on the chapters on Materials and Construction, my deepest appreciation goes to Andrew Roy Addkison, Interior Designer of the California College of Arts and Crafts of Oakland, California.

Contents

YOUR
HOMEMADE
GREENHOUSE
and How to Build It

1 Gardens Under Glass— All Year Long

Years ago only the very wealthy could afford greenhouses, but now there is a greenhouse for everyone's pocketbook. Having a place for plants makes you a gardener year-round rather than just for those few months when outdoor weather is good. A greenhouse filled with colorful flowers and sprouting seeds, whether under plastic or glass, on a roof or underground will fill your soul with warmth inside, even though it may be gray and cold outside. The greenhouse will provide a pleasant retreat from the busy world; you can sneak into your Eden any time and be in a totally new world. Even a window greenhouse can be a valuable addition to the home. And of course a greenhouse will save you money because you can start plants from cuttings, grow herbs and vegetables, and start seeds to get a head start on spring.

Prefabricated greenhouses, available in many sizes and styles, are fine, but building your own greenhouse has four advantages: (1) you can use whatever space is available, from 5 X 10 to 10 X 20 feet; (2) you can use imaginative designs; (3) you can make the greenery part of the house or have a detached unit; (4) and you can use old or new materials. In essence, you can save a great deal of money by doing it yourself. Remember that a prefabricated greenhouse kit is delivered knocked down (KD), so you must put it together as well as supply the foundation (generally a costly project). The greenhouse you design and build yourself (or have built) can be small or large, sophisticated or simple in design, inexpensive or costly. For example, some excellent places for plants cost only $200, and some distinctive and lovely hand-hewn ones cost no more than $500.

greenhouse? First consider these seven questions:

1. Where will it go?
2. What will it be made from?
3. What is the best design for the house?
4. How much money can you spend?
5. What are you going to use it for?
6. Is it to be attached or detached?
7. How much artificial heat will be needed?

To answer these questions, make sketches (you do not have to be an artist) and list the supplies and materials you will need to give you a rough cost estimate. Following are some ideas to get your imagination going. (And drawings are included throughout the book to help you.)

Making Your Own Greenhouse

A greenhouse can be part of any property no matter how limited the outdoor space.

Getting Started

Just how do you go about creating and building your own

Types of Greenhouses

The greenhouse has changed greatly in the past decade and is no longer simply a glass structure. It may be a greenhouse that

SOLAR ANGLES

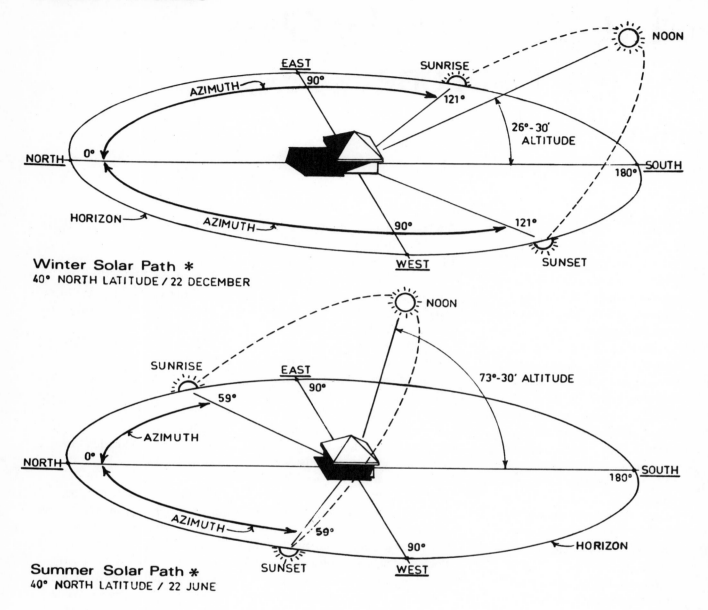

Winter Solar Path *
40° NORTH LATITUDE / 22 DECEMBER

Summer Solar Path *
40° NORTH LATITUDE / 22 JUNE

LATITUDE	SEASON	SUNRISE	SUNSET	AZIMUTH	ALTITUDE
50°	WINTER	8:00	4:00	128°-30'	16°-30'
	SUMMER	4:00	8:00	51°-30'	63°-30'
45°	WINTER	7:40	4:20	124°-30'	21°-30'
	SUMMER	4:20	7:40	55°-30'	68°-30'
* 40°	WINTER	7:30	4:30	121°-0'	26°-30'
	SUMMER	4:30	7:30	59°-0'	73°-30'

LATITUDE	SEASON	SUNRISE	SUNSET	AZIMUTH	ALTITUDE
35°	WINTER	7:10	4:50	119°-0'	31°-30'
	SUMMER	4:50	7:10	61°-30'	78°-30'
30°	WINTER	7:00	5:00	117°-30'	36°-30'
	SUMMER	5:00	7:00	62°-30'	83°-30'
25°	WINTER	6:50	5:10	116°-30'	41°-30'
	SUMMER	5:10	6:50	88°-30'	63°-30'

NOTE: THESE LATITUDES COVER THE CONTINENTAL UNITED STATES. HOURS INDICATED ARE STANDARD TIME. AZIMUTHS ARE AT SUNRISE AND SUNSET, NOON AZIMUTHS ARE ALWAYS 180°. NOON ALTITUDES ARE GIVEN, ALTITUDES AT SUNRISE AND SUNSET ARE ALWAYS 0°.

is partially underground to conserve heat or it may be a dome structure. Your greenhouse may have solar additions (panels) to save heat or if space is at a premium you can install a window greenhouse—these are fine additions for many homes.

In addition to new designs of the structure itself there are new techniques for growing plants: artificial light has gained thousands of followers in the past ten years and growing plants without soil (hydroponically) is becoming popular too.

A greenhouse can be either attached or detached (separate from the house) depending on what you want to use it for. If you are going to display plans the attached unit is better; then the greenery is part of the house, thus increasing the space of your total living area. The attached unit may be adjacent to the living room, offering a pleasant view, off the kitchen, providing a cheerful note on dull days; off the bedroom, becoming a delightful addition to the daily living scheme; or even part of the bathroom, lending a tropical look to the bath and helping to dress up the area considerably.

The attached greenhouse offers easy accessibility to the main house in inclement weather and is an enjoyable place for morning coffee. Finally, the attached unit makes it possible to use existing heating facilities (by adding a duct from the main furnace) and thus cut costs. The disadvantage of the attached unit is that it is always visible to guests and thus must be kept neat to prevent it from being an eyesore.

The detached greenhouse is generally a more personal place,

a place where you can actually work with rather than only display plants. It is the potting shed, the place to propagate plants, the "hospital" for those plants not in their prime. Even though it does not extend your living area, it still can be a retreat from the house if you want to get away from the telephone, relatives, or whatever. And the detached greenhouse unit gives you more scope in

design; an A-frame or a dome, a gazebo-type or an arched structure. (See Chapter 4 for greenhouse designs).

Because this greenhouse acts as its own entity, it does not have to match the main house (the attached unit has to). The detached greenhouse is a workshop of plants that can provide infinite pleasure. Two drawbacks are (1) it must have separate heating, and (2) it is difficult to

When you make your own greenhouse you can build it any size or shape you want to match your home. This small L-shaped unit is in perfect proportion to the house and offers a pleasant view looking into it as well as lovely color when viewed from within the house. Sliding doors and a plastic dome furnish enough light for plants. *(Photo by Clark Photo Graphics).*

get to when weather is bad.

Naturally it would be nice to have both a detached working greenhouse and a display place for plants that is part of the house, but this is rarely feasible because of cost. Why not build one one year and plan the other for the future?

Cost

Because materials are so expensive today, cost is a very important part of building. The average do-it-yourself greenhouse can cost as little as $200 or as much as $2,000. The one I recently added to my kitchen area—simple wood and glass construction, with a tar and gravel roof and domes for light—cost less than $700; similar units can be built easily within this budget. What you cover the basic greenhouse skeleton with determines the actual cost. For example, a covering of flexible plastic for a 10 X 14 greenhouse can cost no more than $60; in rigid fiberglas about $200, in glass or acrylic about $400, and so on. If you can not afford glass or acrylic at the start, go ahead and build the greenhouse skeleton and use a plastic or screen temporary covering; in a year or so (when you have the money), do the permanent installation with glass or plastic.

You can also build a greenhouse from salvaged materials; although it may not be the ultimate in appearance, it will serve to house your plants. A greenhouse of salvaged materials can be built for less than $200 if you

Corrugated fiberglas in combination with wood make this structure a fine area for plants of all kinds. The wood and fiberglas greenhouse is inexpensive, easy to build, and a definite plus on any property. This greenhouse is a detached unit. *(Photo by Matthew Barr).*

Aluminum is the framework for a greenhouse. It is popular because it is easily maintained; this hipped design greenhouse is really a loft unit with a studio below. *(Photo by Pat Matsumoto).*

carefully scout salvage yards.

When you build your own greenhouse, you may have many alternatives, depending on the money available at the time. The initial cost of excavating and foundation should be considered in all greenhouse building; the average concrete footing and foundation will run from $100 to $200, depending on how much labor you do yourself. The more you do, the less it will cost. Concrete footings and foundation details are explained in Chapter 3.

Heating/Water

The amount of artificial heat needed for your greenhouse depends on its size and where you live. In very cold winter regions more heating will be necessary than in, say, southern areas. Greenhouse suppliers have a large selection of heaters, none exorbitant in price and even with the increase in fuel costs, the price of heating the greenhouse will not be expensive. And for those very cold nights that may occur there are some old-fashioned ways of conserving heat within the greenhouse and we talk about these methods as well as specific applications of heaters in Chapter 6.

To determine just how much heat you will need in the greenhouse you will have to know the inside temperature; this means you'll need a thermometer. Find an instrument that is both a thermometer and a hygrometer (that measures moisture in the air) and place it midway on a wall in the greenhouse; this way

The loft greenhouse seen from a distance shows the interesting design. The unit faces south and provides ample light for plants. As an addition to the property it is a totally charming scene. *(Photo by Pat Matsumoto).*

This attached greenhouse is of wood and glass; it is a leanto design using the house wall as a fourth wall. Thus, the view from the kitchen is pleasing and the view from outside equally handsome. The structure faces east and north and this greenhouse owned by the author cost $700 to build. *(Photo by author).*

you will have both temperature and humidity readings at a glance.

Fancy equipment to provide water to your greenhouse is not necessary. In temperate climates you can, of course, use a hose connected to an outside faucet and it will cost nothing. (In climates where winters are severe this would hardly be feasible.) Extending the water line from an existing house line to the greenhouse is not really a costly procedure and a plumber can do it for you. If the greenhouse is detached from the house, the line must be laid beneath the ground (check freezing levels with Building Code offices), and this would involve somewhat more cost than a line from the main house to an attached greenhouse. Either way, a faucet in the greenhouse is necessary and should be considered part of the total greenhouse cost.

Prefabricated Greenhouses

Years ago if you wanted a prefabricated greenhouse you almost had to buy a metal-and-glass structure, usually a lean-to. The detached units then available were often commercial and sterile in appearance. Not so today. Now there is an array of new designs in prefabricated or knocked-down (KD) units. Many manufacturers have gone back to wood framing and there is a choice of cover materials. Domes, arches, and hexagonal shapes are all part of the new greenhouse scene. While the prefabricated unit is convenient—you get all the pieces—you still must put it together yourself and

in the majority of cases you still must have a suitable foundation for the greenhouse which you too supply, so in essence, this is still a homemade project.

If you prefer to buy a greenhouse kit and there are several suitable ones, do add a few handcrafted touches of your own to it. This can be a different kind of door or some overhead beams to give it a personal taste. Also,

with any greenhouse you have, remember that glass is a poor conductor; the greenhouse will be expensive to heat in winter and very hot in summer. Consider using glass in combination with some other material as a covering.

No matter which kind of greenhouse you select, whether it is prefabricated or homemade, and no matter where it is, you

A homemade greenhouse of infinite charm is shown in this attached unit. Redwood is used throughout as building members and plastic fiberglas panels for a ceiling. The casement windows of the house add great beauty to the scene and the lush plantings within the greenhouse always make it an inviting place. Note the wooden door at right, in character to the total picture. *(Photo by Clark Photo Graphics).*

will always be able to grow plants in it. There are plants for every exposure—north, south, east, west—and we discuss them in Chapter 5.

Getting Help

There are some architects who will give you a rough sketch of your own greenhouse design for a minimal fee. However, you have to take it from there. For one of my early greenhouses I hired a local architect who did rough sketches from my pencil drawings for $50 which is hardly exorbitant. Having everything on paper made it easy for me to get started.

Some states' laws say that if you build the greenhouse yourself and the cost of material is, say, under $400, no permit is needed. Other states require a permit for even an outhouse, so check and be sure. In most parts of the country law requires that you install a foundation or footing for your greenhouse. You must conform to building-codes about freezing depth and so forth and it is all for your own good. You can get help by calling your local building-code service (listed in the yellow pages).

Try and get help with digging and pouring the foundation. Working alone is backbreaking; get a handyman or someone to help. Few carpenters are willing to build a greenhouse, and contractors may be too busy building homes, so it might be up to you and in the following chapters we offer help and guidance to get you going with your homemade greenhouse.

An inexpensive wood and plastic-sheet greenhouse can be made in a weekend and serves many purposes. This is simple A-frame construction and affords a place for plants for less than $100. *(Photo by Matthew Barr).*

Looking into a simple wood and plastic greenhouse. *(Photo by Matthew Barr).*

2 Materials For the Greenhouse

You will be using lumber, glass, plastic, and possibly brick for your greenhouse, so it is wise to know something about them. The framing for a greenhouse is generally wood or aluminum and may be covered with flexible plastic, glass, or fiberglas panels. Plastic or glass are generally used for roofs and skylights. Solar panels to conserve heat are also popular. Floors are usually made of concrete or brick. The end of this chapter has tables for your convenience: types of plastic covering, aspects of glass use, and charts on lumber specifications.

Wood

Wood is a basic building material; it is easy to work with, can be cut and sawed, nailed and drilled by even the average person. It is available in a mind-boggling array of sizes, species, and grades. You should be acquainted with some of the basic wood information because wood will be the framing for your greenhouse unless you use prefab metal units or salvaged materials. Recently there has been a return to wood because it

is more charming and better looking than metal, which can be quite sterile in appearance. With wood, you can used curved lines if necessary and have more latitude in design, especially in regards to greenhouse construction.

Woods are generally divided into two types: hardwood, such as oak, maple, beech; and softwoods, such as cedar, redwood, and pine. Hardwood, more durable and harder to work with than softwood, is usually used for floors or furniture construction. Softwoods are easy to work with and so far for our purposes are the best materials.

Redwood and cedar heartwood lumber is more resistant to decay than most other woods. It can take an awful lot of moisture and yet last for years; has an inherent acid preservative, and is more termite proof than most woods. Douglas fir is good too, and cypress (if you can find it) has exceptional qualities. Generally, even with redwood, wood preservatives or paint will be needed to further ensure long-lasting qualities. There are various grades of lumber to consider; see the charts at the end of this section.

WOOD PRESERVATIVES

Preservatives will lengthen the life of any wood because they will protect the woods from moisture. There are many wood preservatives available at hardware and paint stores sold under a variety of trade names. They make wood almost perfectly resistant to water penetration. Wood preservatives can injure skin, so handle them carefully: wear gloves, try not to get any on your hands, and follow to the letter the directions on the can.

A good quality paint will further protect wood. Because there are so many paints available, it is impossible to discuss them here. Tell your paint dealer that the paint will be used for greenhouse construction and let him guide you accordingly.

BUYING LUMBER

If at all possible, design the greenhouse so the length of lumber parts—rafters, beams, and posts—are in even numbers because lumber is sold on the even inch. Always use, if you can, even-numbered lumber. Odd sizes are not always in stock and have to be cut from even sizes, in which case you must pay for

BASIC GLASS INSTALLATION - WOOD

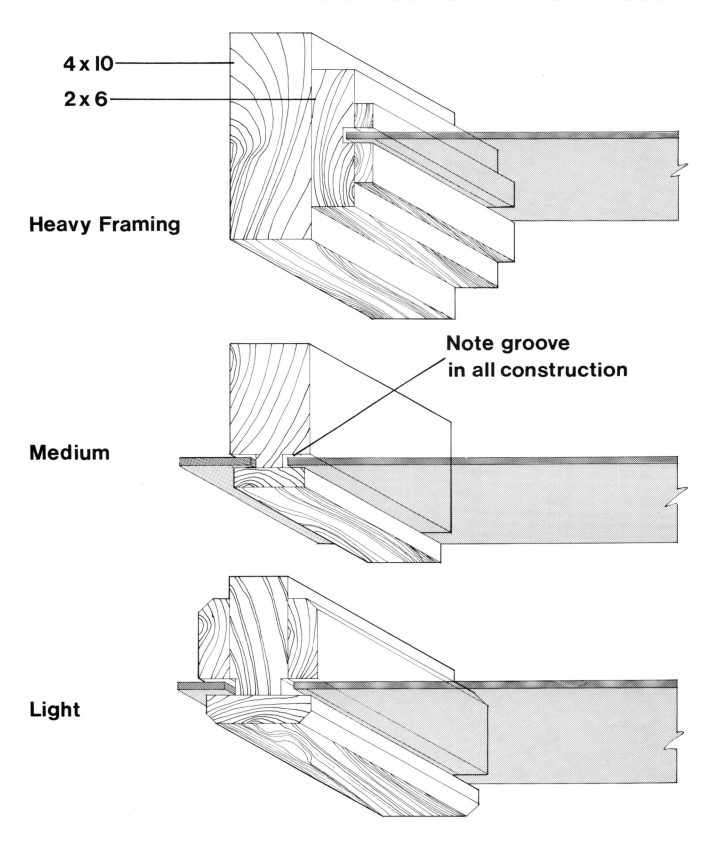

4 x 10

2 x 6

Heavy Framing

**Note groove
in all construction**

Medium

Light

BASIC GLASS INSTALLATION - METAL

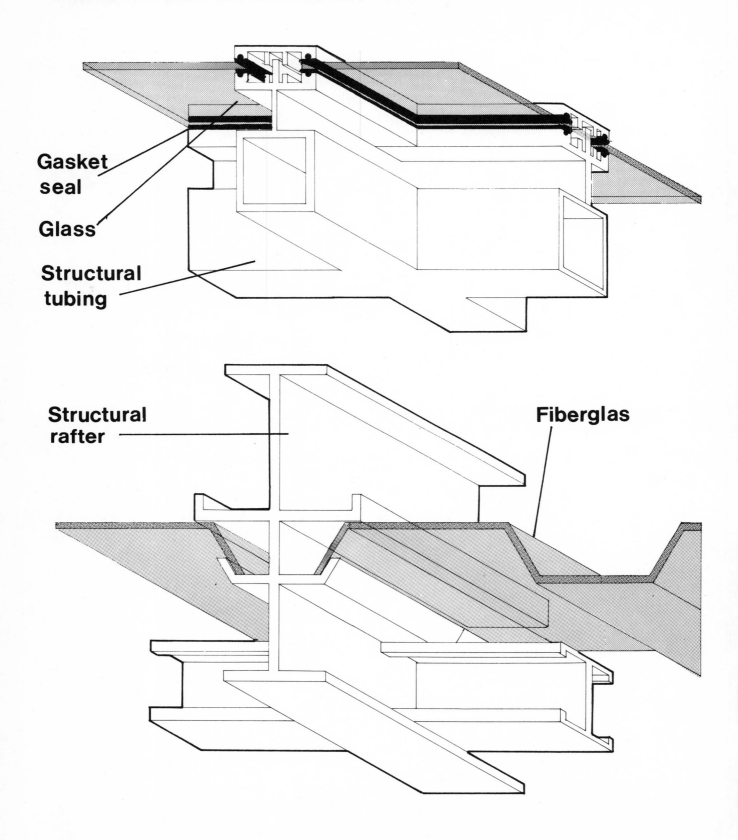

Gasket seal

Glass

Structural tubing

Structural rafter

Fiberglas

Standard Dimensions of Surfaced Lumber

	Surfaced Actual Size	
Size to Order	Unseasoned	Dry
2 X 3	1 9/16 X 2 1/16	1 1/2 X 2 1/2
2 X 4	1 9/16 X 3 9/16	1 1/2 X 3 1/2
2 X 6	1 9/16 X 5 5/8	1 1/2 X 5 1/2
2 X 8	1 9/16 X 7 1/2	1 1/2 X 7 1/4
2 X 10	1 9/16 X 9 1/2	1 1/2 X 9 1/4
2 X 12	1 9/16 X 11 1/2	1 1/2 X 11 1/4

Kinds of Lumber

GRADES	REDWOOD CEDAR	RED CEDAR	DOUGLAS FIR
Top grade; expensive: used mostly for cabinetry. Structural members for heavy construction.	All heart	C and better finishes	C and better finishes
Excellent for most uses; only slight defects	Select heart	C finishes	C finishes
Suitable for general construction; has some knots and defects; economical, but should be painted	Construction cart	Merchantable construction	Construction

Note: Lumber comes in grades such as A, B, C, D; A denotes top quality.

the longer size and the cutting of the wood.

When you design the roof, know at the start what roofing material you will be using; glass, acrylic, or fiberglas. Spacing and structural support depend on the weight. When buying lumber, specify exactly what grade you want and the size and length needed. State quantity first, type of wood, size, and then length.

Glass

For years the standard greenhouse glass sizes were 16 X 20 and 18 X 24. Today, these sizes are still used, but they are no longer mandatory.

Greenhouse glass is designated SSB (single strength B grade) or DSB (double strength B grade). SSB is 1/16 inch thick; DSB is 1/8 inch thick. The B designation does not mean that much as opposed to the A or top-quality type. DSB and SSB (commonly called window glass) is available on the even inch in boxes of 50 or 100 square feet, so a box of glass 16 X 20 would contain fourteen pieces (lites). Greenhouse glass may also be 3/16 or even 7/32 inch thick; naturally these thicknesses weigh and cost more.

Glass *must* be glazed properly. The glass must fit precisely the aluminum or wooden opening.

Glazing compound is put around the edges to seal the glass, and generally a moulding (or a capping if aluminum is used) is set in place. If properly installed, glass is leakproof, which is of utmost importance in greenhouse construction.

In some states, if you use glass to ground units, you will have to use tempered or wire glass at ground level or moullion bars at least 16 inches above ground level for safety reasons. Tempered glass is five times as strong as standard glass and comes in various thicknesses: 3/16, 7/32, and 1/34 inch. Tempered glass breaks into small pieces, thus avoiding serious accidents. Wire glass is clear glass with wire inserts. If it breaks, the glass adheres to the wire rather than cracking into large pieces.

GLAZING COMPOUNDS

There is a host of new glazing compounds on the market. But investigate before you buy because the right glazing material can mean the difference between a lot of maintenance or little maintenance. The newer compounds are hard on the outside but remain pliable inside, which is a definite plus. They also have a longer life and are extremely easy to install with a glazing gun.

The mastic-type compounds are good, but the plastic types are even better. Putty, which for so many years has been used to install glass, should be avoided because it becomes brittle and then falls away in a year or so. And using a putty knife to glaze with, is much more difficult than using a glazing gun.

Redwood has been used extensively for this small greenhouse. Note that the window members shown are rabbetted (notched) to provide space for glass. This type of construction also eliminates leakage possibilities. To assure moisture from entering wood, all wooden members were given a protective clear coating and then two coats of paint. *(Photo by author).*

Plastic

FLEXIBLE

Polyethylene, the most used flexible plastic, comes in cones of 2, 4, and 6 mil thicknesses, in a variety of widths. The heavier the plastic, the longer its life. Do not expect any polyethylene sking to last more than 1 year.

Vinyl plastic comes in 8 mil thicknesses, in 36, 48, and 60 inch widths. It is more costly than polyethylene but lasts about twice as long. However, in extreme cold it becomes brittle.

Polyester plastic is available in 3 or 5 mil thicknesses. This is about the best flexible plastic, sometimes lasting as long as 3 years. It requires overlapping and should be stretched as tightly as possible on the frame to eliminate noise rattle.

FIBERGLAS

The fiberglas sheet panel, corrugated or flat, is a simple answer to installation and cost for greenhouse roofing or siding. Also, it is easy to work with because it is lightweight, and can be drilled and sawed, even by the novice. Its one disadvantage is that it is not always esthetically pleasing, but if properly framed and detailed, it can be quite handsome.

Panels are either brightly colored or translucent; either type admits sufficient subdued light for most plants, which is excellent for plant growth. I prefer the translucent panels because they are more natural looking, and the corrugated panel is easier to install than the flat one.

Because the corrugated panel is the most popular, we shall outline its installation; except for the overlapping principle, most other fiberglas panels can be installed in the same manner.

The 26-inch panel is the most common size; this provides a 2-inch overlap on rafters spaced 2 feet on centers. Use wood members to support the panels along the seams. You should also use cross bracing, every 5 feet between the rafters, to support the panels so they do not sag. Thus an eggcrate-type framing system ideally suits panels.

As previously mentioned, try to build your greenhouse roof or sides with standard-sized materials to avoid time-consuming cutting. If you have to cut, use a fine-toothed hand saw. Fiberglas panels can be nailed, but do use the nails made especially for fiberglas; they have a rubber washer that eliminates the possibility of crazing around the nail hole. Nail panels every 12 inches, driving the nails through the crowns rather than the valleys of the corrugation.

Glass Data

MATERIAL	THICKNESS, TYPE	INSTALLATION	STANDARD SIZE	REMARKS
Window glass DSB	1/8 inch thick rolled glass	Glazing compound and clips	16 X 18 in 2 inch increments	Best for average size greenhouse; maximum size 30 X 40
Window glass SSB	1/16 inch rolled glass	Glazing compound and clips	16 X 18 in 2 inch increments	Cheaper than above but not as good; maximum size 24 X 30
Wire glass	1/4 inch thick; wire embedded	Glazing compound and clips	4 to 12 feet long, in 2 inch increments	Necessary for skylights; looks good. Can be used in any size.
Tempered glass	1/4 inch thick; clear	Glazing compound and clips	Many sizes (check with dealer)	Necessary for skylights. Sometimes warps; stay with small sizes.

Glass is used in combination with plastic windows in this greenhouse. The small panes of glass are easy to install and the egg-crate framing adds charm to the unit. *(Photo by Matthew Barr).*

PLASTIC SCREEN GREENHOUSE

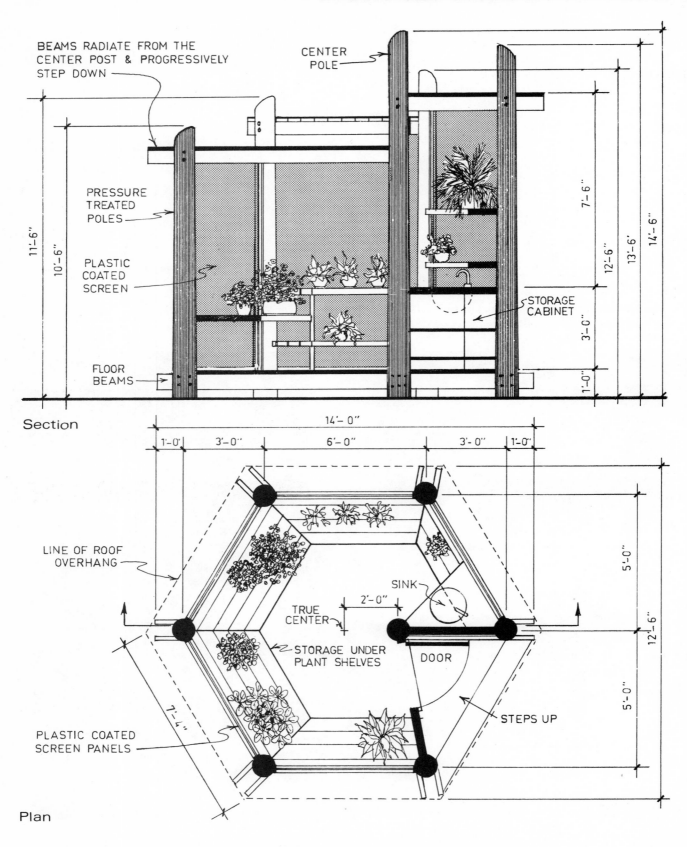

BEAMS RADIATE FROM THE CENTER POST & PROGRESSIVELY STEP DOWN

CENTER POLE

PRESSURE TREATED POLES

PLASTIC COATED SCREEN

7'-6"

14'-6"

13'-6"

12'-6"

STORAGE CABINET

11'-6"

10'-6"

3'-0"

FLOOR BEAMS

1'-0"

Section

14'-0"

1'-0" 3'-0" 6'-0" 3'-0" 1'-0"

LINE OF ROOF OVERHANG

SINK

5'-0"

TRUE CENTER

2'-0"

STORAGE UNDER PLANT SHELVES

DOOR

12'-6"

STEPS UP

7'-4"

5'-0"

PLASTIC COATED SCREEN PANELS

Plan

GREENHOUSE WITH ACRYLIC

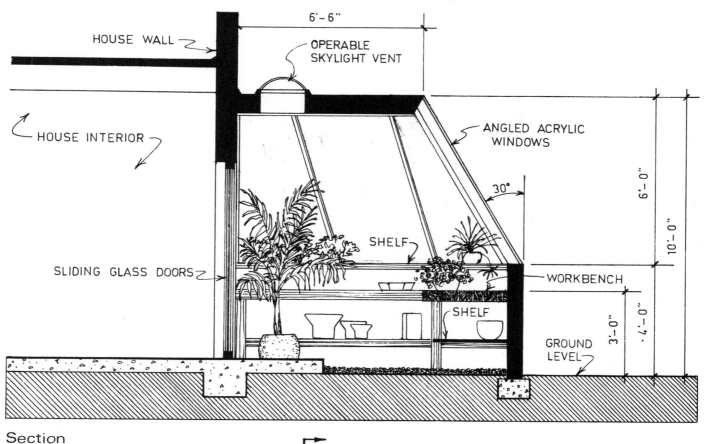

HOUSE WALL

HOUSE INTERIOR

SLIDING GLASS DOORS

6'-6"

OPERABLE SKYLIGHT VENT

ANGLED ACRYLIC WINDOWS

30°

SHELF

WORKBENCH

SHELF

GROUND LEVEL

6'-0"

10'-0"

3'-0"

4'-0"

Section

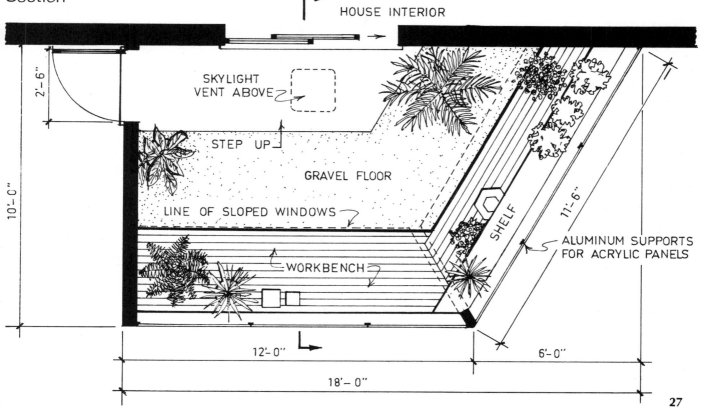

HOUSE INTERIOR

2'-6"

10'-0"

SKYLIGHT VENT ABOVE

STEP UP

GRAVEL FLOOR

LINE OF SLOPED WINDOWS

WORKBENCH

SHELF

11'-6"

ALUMINUM SUPPORTS FOR ACRYLIC PANELS

12'-0"

6'-0"

18'-0"

CORRUGATED FIBERGLAS GREENHOUSE

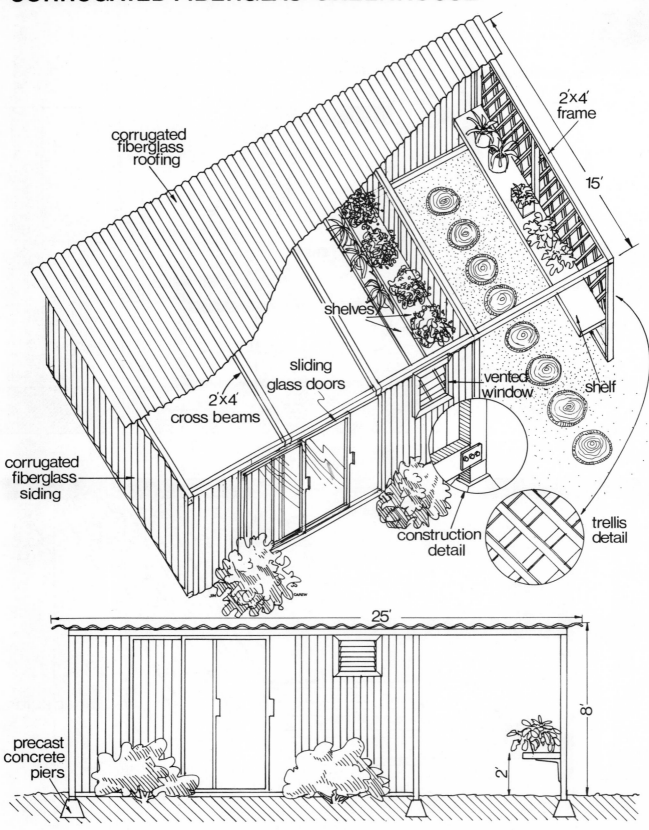

corrugated fiberglass roofing

2'x4' frame

15'

shelves

sliding glass doors

2'x4' cross beams

vented window

shelf

corrugated fiberglass siding

construction detail

trellis detail

25'

precast concrete piers

8'

2'

Plastic Covering for Skeleton Framing

MATERIAL	DESCRIPTION	INSTALLATION	STANDARD SIZES	REMARKS
Flexible plastic	Almost clear	Stapling gun	24 to 48 inch width rolls	Temporary
Fiberglas panels	Strong rigid sheets; flat or corrugated; in colors or almost clear	Nailed or screwed in	20 to 36 inch wide, 60, 72 or 96 inches long	Can last several years
Saran shade cloth	Plastic, with many densities	Tacks or stapling gun	24 to 60 inch widths	Temporary
Plastic screen	Wire embedded in plastic	Staple gun	35 inch width rolls	Can last a year or more; looks okay
Aluminum and plastic	Gray, plastic-coated aluminum wires	Nailed to wood frame	24 to 48 inch width rolls	Looks okay; can last about a year

Plastic flexible covering can be used for greenhouse skeletons but at best are only temporary and will have to be replaced with other materials. Still, if money is short this is the way to go because flexible plastic is inexpensive and does offer some protection from the elements. *(Photo by author).*

This small L-shaped greenhouse is glazed with flat fiberglas panels of natural color; combined with the white painted wood framing it is esthetically pleasing and functional. *(Photo by Clark Photo Graphics).*

You can also use special wood screws (sold at dealers) instead of nails. Be sure and first apply mastic sealant between the panels whether using nails or screws.

Occasionally hose down panels with clear water to eliminate dirt and soot buildup. You can resurface the panels by rubbing them with pads of soft steel wool, working lengthwise along the corrugations. When panels are thoroughly dry, apply a liquid resin that dries to a smooth, tough finish which provides a strong outer skin over the original surface.

Corrugated fiberglas panels are used for this detached greenhouse. Overlapped and on redwood frames they make an excellent covering; these are light green in color. *(Photo by Matthew Barr).*

3 Construction Of the Greenhouse

Whether you design and build your own room or have a designer or contractor do it for you, some basic information about construction will provide you with a background so you can construct a functional room. The following information will enable you to talk knowingly to carpenters or contractors and/or show you how to build your own room.

Footings

First you must consider footings and foundations because they anchor the greenhouse to the ground (a footing is part of the foundation). Footings can be of slab construction, a footings-and-foundation wall, used with a masonry wall, concrete tubes, or precast piers. Several types of footings are shown in Drawings. Designs may vary depending upon where you live and building codes, but the following general plan can be used:

1. Drive twelve stakes or four batten boards 3 to 8 feet from the proposed corners. Lay out the exact plan of the building with string from stake to stake or board to board.

2. Dig a trench approximately 2 feet wide and a minimum of 1 foot deep (or whatever building codes advise) around the perimeter of the proposed site.

3. Decide what height the foundation footing will be, and then use a level to make sure all batten boards or stakes are on the same level.

4. Rent foundation framing equipment, or use 3/4-inch plywood. The width of the footing should be 8 inches or whatever local building codes require.

5. If the room is to be a heavy structure, reinforce footings with steel rods inlaid horizontally and vertically. Pound the vertical rods into the ground between the foundation framing and then tie the horizontal rods (use wires) to the vertical ones.

6. Leave 1/4- to 1/2 inch D anchor bolts (available at lumber yards) protruding from the top of the footing as a base for nailing in upright members. The length of the bolt depends upon the size of the bearing plate you use, but be sure to allow for a longer rather than a short bolt. Lay the bearing plate approximately 1 inch inside the outside line of the footing.

7. Apply mastic to the top of the footing to stop capillary action.

8. Be sure there is adequate drainage. Leave 3-inch holes in the foundation based about every 6 feet so water can run off to a lower grade.

9. For outside drainage, place drain tiles at the base and through the footings, on 4 to 6 inches of rough gravel.

10. For inside drainage, plan a floor drain (optional). Before floor is installed, locate the drainage heads in a low area. The drain-pipe should extend all around the exterior of the room at the base of the footing in trench.

As mentioned, the above information is for general footing and foundation work. You can in some instances use precast concrete piers (sold at suppliers) as footings for say, lightweight greenhouses, and then the flooring material would be cinders, gravel, or earth.

The Frame

The frame or skeleton of your greenhouse is your next con-

CONCRETE DETAILS

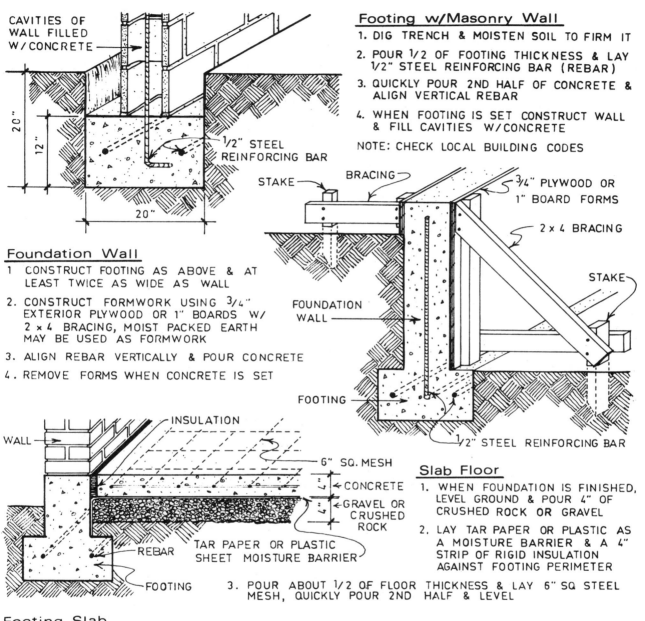

CAVITIES OF WALL FILLED W/CONCRETE

20"

12"

½" STEEL REINFORCING BAR

20"

Foundation Wall

1 CONSTRUCT FOOTING AS ABOVE & AT LEAST TWICE AS WIDE AS WALL

2. CONSTRUCT FORMWORK USING ¾" EXTERIOR PLYWOOD OR 1" BOARDS W/ 2 × 4 BRACING, MOIST PACKED EARTH MAY BE USED AS FORMWORK

3. ALIGN REBAR VERTICALLY & POUR CONCRETE

4. REMOVE FORMS WHEN CONCRETE IS SET

Footing w/Masonry Wall

1. DIG TRENCH & MOISTEN SOIL TO FIRM IT

2. POUR ½ OF FOOTING THICKNESS & LAY ½" STEEL REINFORCING BAR (REBAR)

3. QUICKLY POUR 2ND HALF OF CONCRETE & ALIGN VERTICAL REBAR

4. WHEN FOOTING IS SET CONSTRUCT WALL & FILL CAVITIES W/CONCRETE

NOTE: CHECK LOCAL BUILDING CODES

STAKE   BRACING   ¾" PLYWOOD OR 1" BOARD FORMS

2 × 4 BRACING

FOUNDATION WALL

STAKE

FOOTING

½" STEEL REINFORCING BAR

WALL   INSULATION

6" SQ. MESH

CONCRETE

GRAVEL OR CRUSHED ROCK

REBAR

TAR PAPER OR PLASTIC SHEET MOISTURE BARRIER

FOOTING

Slab Floor

1. WHEN FOUNDATION IS FINISHED, LEVEL GROUND & POUR 4" OF CRUSHED ROCK OR GRAVEL

2. LAY TAR PAPER OR PLASTIC AS A MOISTURE BARRIER & A 4" STRIP OF RIGID INSULATION AGAINST FOOTING PERIMETER

3. POUR ABOUT ½ OF FLOOR THICKNESS & LAY 6" SQ STEEL MESH, QUICKLY POUR 2ND HALF & LEVEL

Footing Slab

1. DIG TRENCH & LEVEL FLOOR AREA

2. SET FORMWORK AROUND PERIMETER

3. POUR 4" OF GRAVEL OR CRUSHED ROCK COVER W/ TAR PAPER OR PLASTIC SHEET

4. POUR CONCRETE & LAY REINFORCING BARS & STEEL MESH AT APPROPIATE LEVELS

5. LEVEL FLOOR & REMOVE FORMS WHEN CONCRETE IS SET

2 × 6 FORM   6" SQ. MESH

STAKE & BRACING

12"

12"

10"

TAR PAPER OR PLASTIC OVER GRAVEL

struction consideration. You can use the traditional aluminum, but it is sterile looking. Some manufacturers of prefabricated greenhouses have started offering anodized colored aluminum, which is somewhat better. The structural elements of these prefabs are made of aluminum alloy or hot-dip galvanized steel. You do not have to paint aluminum, and the metal does not deteriorate. However, besides its sterile look, aluminum has another drawback: heat loss is greater than with wood, so heating an aluminum greenhouse can be expensive.

Thus, there has been a return to the use of wood. An objection to wood for a greenhouse has been that it rots because of the water and humidity. But today's excellent wood preservatives and paints overcome most problems. Definitely consider building your greenhouse of redwood, cedar, cypress, or Douglas fir.

The framing for your greenhouse is actually the walls, and knowing the difference between a bearing and nonbearing wall is vital before you start any building project. Bearing parts carry the weight of the structure; nonbearing walls do not. Thus, all exterior walls that run perpendicular to ceiling and floor joists are bearing.

The frame of your greenhouse should be made from seasoned lumber (for durability) that holds nails readily and does not warp or twist. Douglas fir is often used, although redwood is the best. There are two kinds of framing involved in greenhouse construction: western and balloon. Western framing is easy to build, works well because it

resists shrinkage, and is preferred for simple greenhouses. Balloon framing is used where masonry covers walls because settlement at joints will not be as severe as with western framing. Mud sills, sole plates, headers for window framing, and wall studs are the basic components of framing. Roof framing includes rafters, beams, and posts.

POSTS

Generally, use 4 X 4 inch redwood posts (vertical supports) for

very large structures; use larger posts (6 X 6 inch) to support heavy roof loads and still maintain post spacing. Heavy roof loads must be considered in any area with heavy snows.

To determine how much weight your posts will hold, calculate the area of the roof supported by each post. Take the area bounded by lines drawn halfway between the post and any adjoining post or wall. Then multiply the area by roof-loading figures for your specific area (get

Footings and foundations are needed for most greenhouses, or at least concrete piers for lightweight ones. Note reinforcing rods used. Concrete will be poured flush with wood framing. This foundation was for a greenhouse 20 x 26 feet. Smaller units would not need such extensive walls. *(Photo by Dilday).*

BASIC CONSTUCTION - FOOTINGS AND RAFTERS

A **Footings**

1 CONCRETE COLLAR
2 POST ANCHOR
3 NAILING BLOCK
4 DRIFT PIN

B **Rafters**

1 TOENAIL
2 NOTCH RAFTERS
3 LEDGER
4 TOENAIL
5 JOIST HANGER

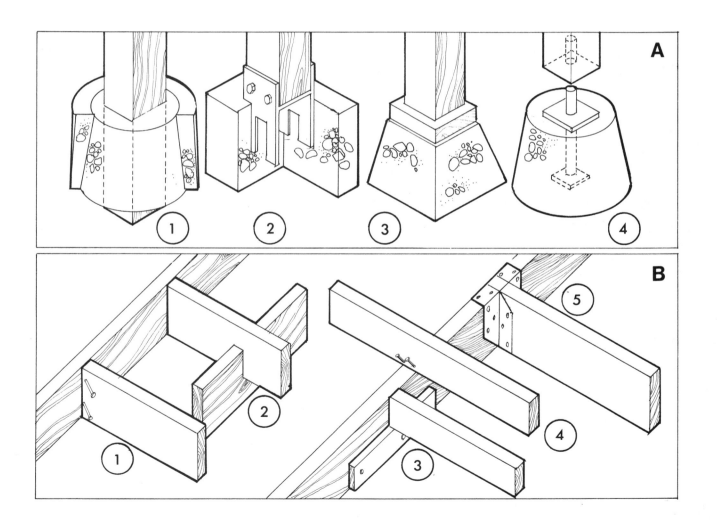

these from local building offices). For example, in most climates (but not all) a 40-pound per square foot load will provide a safe load figure.

BEAMS

To determine the size beam (horizontal support) needed for greenhouse construction, use the following rule of thumb: for a 4 X 4-foot span, a 4 X 4-inch beam is fine; for a 6-foot span use a 4-X 6-inch beam; for an 8-foot span use a 4 X 8-inch beam, and so on. You must use heavy beams for greenhouses with glass because glass is heavy. Lighter beams are fine for plastic covered greenhouses or small ones. Because each climate varies as to the amount of snow load, as previously mentioned check local building departments to determine the necessary dimensions for beams.

RAFTERS

To determine the size of the rafters needed, take the length of the rafter and the center-to-center spacing. A 2- X 4-inch rafter on a 16-inch center is fine, or use a 2 X 6 X 8 on 24-inch centers. Always try to use a select heart California redwood or Douglas fir. These woods are strong and smooth and free of ragged surfaces where fungus and rot could collect from excessive moisture which is prevalent in all greenhouses.

Roofing

The roof, one of the most important parts of a greenhouse,

may be gabled, A-framed, vaulted, saw toothed, or more commonly, a lean-to, placed at an angle against a house wall. If the roof is all glass, it can admit too much direct sun and burn plants, so use only about 30 percent glass in the roof. This admits plenty of light for plants. The rest of the roof can be tar-and-gravel or shingles or any other roofing material.

The glass area may be glass panes set in wood panels, commercial or custom-made skylights, or plastic domes. Proper installation of glass in wood panels is difficult because leakage always seems a problem. Even custom-made, these units are apt to leak so be forwarned. Also remember that building codes require tempered or wire glass in roof construction.

If you use glass in wood panels you will have to make your own or have them custom-made by a mill house. Commercial skylights are at building suppliers (see yellow pages of your phone book), and plastic domes (which are generally leakproof) are at glass stores. Ask for brochures on these materials to determine sizes available.

A good roof for greenhouse construction is one made of 2 X 4 redwood rafters, rabetted (notched out) to accommodate glass panes. Use 16 X 20, 18 X 20, or 20 X 24-inch glass; anything larger will be difficult to handle. Prime the wood members with a preservative. When this is dry, put caulking compound into a squeegee-type plunger; pump the caulking compound along the V shoulder of the wooden member. Now lay glass into the caulking bed, carefully using your palms.

Leave a 1/16-inch space on each side between glass and wood so the caulking will squeeze up at the juncture of wood and glass as the pane is being set in place. Scrape away excess material. Put in lathing over this; nail in the lathing.

Overlapping panes of glass are frequently used in greenhouse construction, but this is bothersome, ugly looking, but causes less leakage. Make individual framing if you want for each piece of glass; this way you can dictate the size of the glass and use any size you want rather than being restricted to specific sizes, although some leakage might occur.

Always pitch roofs slightly so excess water drains freely.

Skylights, (glass and plastic)

Glass skylights come in a range of shapes: single pitched, double pitched, hipped, gabled, hipped with ridge ventilators, and flat. The glass is usually glazed in metal, but wooden members can be used instead. Commercial skylights are available, but generally you will have to have skylights made to size by sheet-metal houses to accommodate specific needs. As a rule, custom-made skylights are expensive, so if at all possible use commercial industrial factory skylights, which are cheaper. You can do your own glazing; just remember to use tempered or wire glass, as explained previously, to prevent accidents. (Exceptions are prefabricated greenhouses, which come with standard glass.) Many

ROOF VARIATIONS

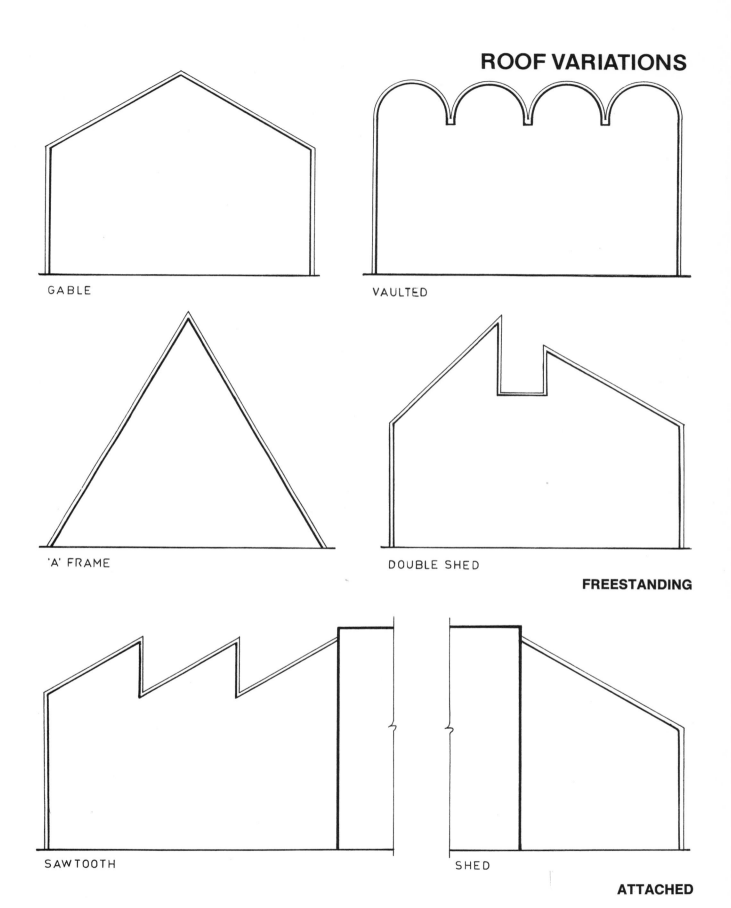

GABLE

VAULTED

'A' FRAME

DOUBLE SHED

FREESTANDING

SAWTOOTH

SHED

ATTACHED

SKYLIGHT DESIGNS - PLASTIC

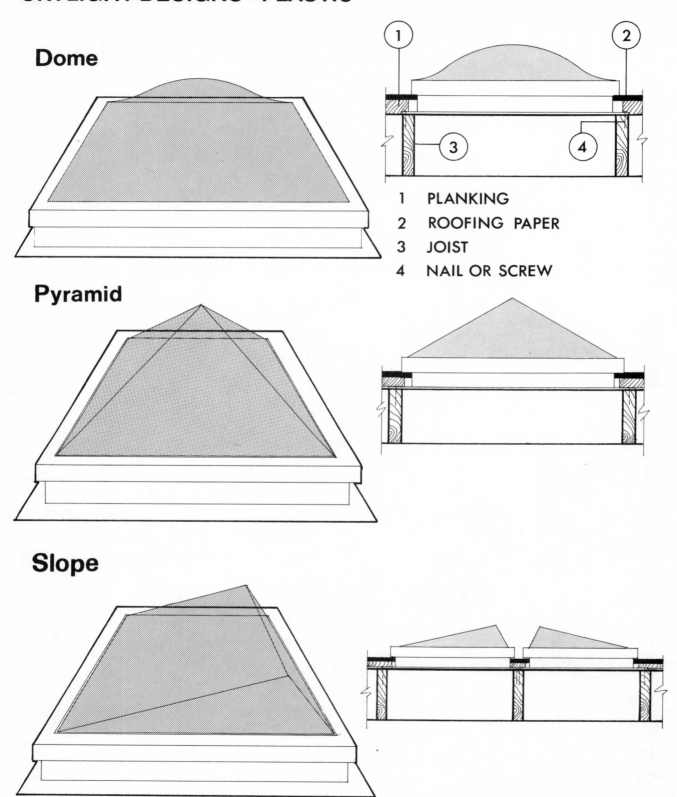

Dome

Pyramid

Slope

1   PLANKING
2   ROOFING PAPER
3   JOIST
4   NAIL OR SCREW

skylights leak, so glaze very carefully. Install glass on a caulking bed in the precast frame. Read instructions on caulking compound packages carefully and heed them. If your glass is 1/4-inch thick, a suitable 1/4-inch groove must be part of the skylight members.

Installing a glass skylight frame is not easy because you must be precise. Leave an opening in the roof to accommodate the outside dimensions of the frame. Put in wooden headers and blocking, usually 2 X 4s but heavier if the skylight is large.

Fit the skylight over this wooden frame, making sure it is flush so no air enters. It is important that your framing (blocks and header) are as absolutely square as the skylight. Apply mastic or caulking at the roof line, put the skylight in place with screws.

The preformed or molded plastic skylight is a handsome addition and provides maximum light for plants. Acrylic plastic is available in several shapes and sizes; it is impervious to weather, lightweight, and easy to build with. Acrylic plastic skylights are domed, right angled,

peaked, or triangular. The dome shape comes in 37 X 37 standard, 48 X 48, and so forth. The other designs may not be in stock but can be ordered by your glass or plastic dealer.

For an average greenhouse, say, 10 X 15 feet, you can get plenty of light with only two 37-inch domes. The larger the greenhouse the more domes you will need; the design of your greenery will dictate what shape to use.

Lathing

Lathing deserves a special section because it is such a versatile and inexpensive material to use for greenhouse construction. Laths are wooden strips used primarily as a surface for plastering. They are sold in bundles; redwood lathing is generally available in most areas. When covered with flexible plastic, lathing supplies a convenient temporary greenhouse at low cost. Because laths can be spaced to your dimensions and easily sawed, you can construct many different designs, from a square to a sophisticated dome.

Lathing is lightweight, so extensive foundation work is not required. Simple footings available at lumber yards can be used, with 4 X 4 posts as main supports spaced 24 inches on center (depending on the size of the greenhouse). The most satisfactory lathing is either redwood or red cedar heartwood because these woods are naturally weather resistant, do not need painting, and their straight grains make them less liable to warp or split. Common lath thicknesses are

Rafter and ceiling supports are shown in this photo. Treated Douglas fir was used. The egg-crate design of the ceiling makes application of fiberglas easy. *(Photo by Matthew Barr).*

Basic greenhouse construction is well displayed here: beams, rafters, and a slightly pitched ceiling so there is proper water runoff. The foundation in this case is concrete blocks. *(Photo by Matthew Barr).*

This is simple A frame construction; the skeleton is then set on a foundation of concrete block (at left) and the greenhouse can be glazed with plastic or glass. This is simple inexpensive building. *(Photo by author).*

about 3/8 X 1-5/8 inches, sold in lengths of 4, 6, and 8 feet in bundles of fifty pieces. Battens, which can also be used for lightweight greenhouse construction, are somewhat larger than laths: 1/4 to 3/4 inch in thickness, with widths of 2 to 3 inches, usually available in 6 or 8 foot lengths in bundles of thirty pieces. Lathing or battens can be put in place over regular post and beam construction.

Connecting to the House

For lean-to greenhouses the house wall is the fourth wall, or use the eave or the roof as a connecting point. Remember to place the roof line high enough so it clears swinging door and windows. If the eaves are low to the ground and you are using 6-or 8-inch rafters, you may have to attach your overhead above the eave to gain needed clearance.

Attaching to the house wall itself is the general procedure and the easiest method. Carefully remove exterior finish of wall; securely fasten a long board (ledger) to the wall studs.

Rest the rafter ends on top of the ledger and then toenail them in place; a ledger can be 2 X 6 or heavier if necessary. The rafters have to support both their own weight over open space without sagging and the weight of the roof, so they must be strong and sturdy. For example, a 2 X 4 is not heavy enough to hold the weight. A 2 X 6 or, better, a 2 X 8 is more satisfactory. The rafters will also require bracing at each end and in the center to keep them in line so they do not twist or sag; use two 2 X 6 or 2 X 8 blocks.

Remember to slope the roof so water can roll off. For roof slope figure 1/4 inch per every foot. Cut a triangular piece off the rafter end where it rests on the ledger strip and on the beam. Cut out the notches and fit the rafter in place to see if it is right. Use the first rafter as a template to make the others. Toenail the rafter in place, and use a sealer preservative at the joint before nailing the rafter in place. Put in metal flashing (sheet metal or weather stripping) at the joint. Now replace house wall boards over flashing to meet roof of greenhouse.

If you are using skylights in the roof, follow this procedure. Most skylights on lean-to greenhouses cover three roof joists (beams); remove these joists and reframe with a header (beam) and blocking (a support). Make an opening about 1/4 inch larger than the metal part of the skylight; this opening should accommodate your wall board. Now install vertical 2 X 4s between the ceiling and rafters; cut the 2 X 4s at an angle so they fit against the rafters. Nail together the 2 X 4s and rafters and toenail to joints. Pull back and cut away the roofing material—shingles or otherwise. Put wallboard in place on each side from finished roof to ceiling level. Install the plastic fixture on the roof and nail it in place, or fasten according to manufacturer's directions. Caulk and seal it. For flat roofs, use only headers and blocking. Set the skylight unit over headers and blocking, nail in place, and seal with caulking.

Doors and Sliding Units

Doors for greenhouses need not be elaborate or special; standard sized wooden doors (at dealers) can be used satisfactorily. Or if you want more charm in the greenhouse, use a casement-type door. The framing and hanging of the door (once left to professionals) is no longer a problem because factory-built, prehung door frames are at dealers. And framing for the door is simple to install.

Fiberglas ceilings eliminate any need for domes or skylights and yet affords plenty of light for plants. It is an inexpensive and good way to build the ceiling. Always pitch the roof slightly to allow for water runoff. *(Photo by Clark Photo Graphics).*

The first thing to remember when framing your door is that the framing must be square. Slip the pre-hung door, which is like a box, into a stud-frame opening (depending on door size) and then secure it. You will also need a still and threshold for the door; the sill slopes away from the door at the base to keep out water, and the threshold covers the opening between the bottom edge of the door and the floor.

Above the door, put in place a header, usually two 2 X 4s on edge, or use a 4 X 4. Place trimmer studs against the full-length framing studs on each side of the door. To hang the door, be sure the stud opening is slightly larger than the size of the prehung frame to allow space to shim the frame so it is exactly plumb and level. (Shims are shingles or wedges of wood driven between the frame and trimmer and also below the header.) After framing is nailed in place, break off the shim flush with the trimmer studs. Nail casing trim against the opening to both the trimmer studs and the frame edges. Miter the mouldings at the top corners.

Sliding metal or wooden doors are popular and come in a wide range of sizes and quality. Sliding doors have either bottom or top rollers. To order your doors, tell the dealer the size of the opening. Like a standard door, sliders need trimmer studs on each side and a header on top, generally a 4

In this greenhouse glass custom made skylights are used to provide light for plants. Skylight framing can be seen at upper right. *(Photo by author).*

X 4, or heavier if the span is long.

Set the door frame in position so it is against the trimmer stud. Put screws in loosely through the frame into the studs and also into the header beam so the door is in place while your make necessary adjustments. There should be about 1/2 inch space between the door frame and the header, a ¼ inch between sides and studs. Now determine which side of the opening is the locking side; shim between the frame and trimmer stud on that side. Once the blocking and shimming is one, tighten and secure the frame in place.

Flooring

CONCRETE

Concrete is an economical and durable floor material because it resists stains and water and will retain heat. To build your concrete floor you will need wooden forms, that is, forms to hold the concrete until it sets. You can build your own forms, but it is easier to rent them, or use steel stake forms. Put the forms in place absolutely level, with the top wood board floor level. Reinforcing steel rods must go around the footing; these support the weight of the building and anchor it.

Always install a gravel base; this provides a solid level for concrete to rest on and facilitates drainage. Install over the gravel a plastic sheet; this will act as a vapor barrier. Make the floor at least 4 inches thick and reinforce it with steel mesh. Be sure the ground is absolutely level or concrete may crack eventually. Use

Concrete pavers make an easy and economical flooring almost impervious to destruction. Further they are easily installed and water evaporating on concrete provides humidity in the greenhouse. *(Photo by Matthew Barr).*

A brick floor is always charming and adds beauty to a greenhouse. It is somewhat more expensive than concrete pavers but does make a durable greenhouse flooring. *(Photo by Matthew Barr).*

GREENHOUSE LAYOUT

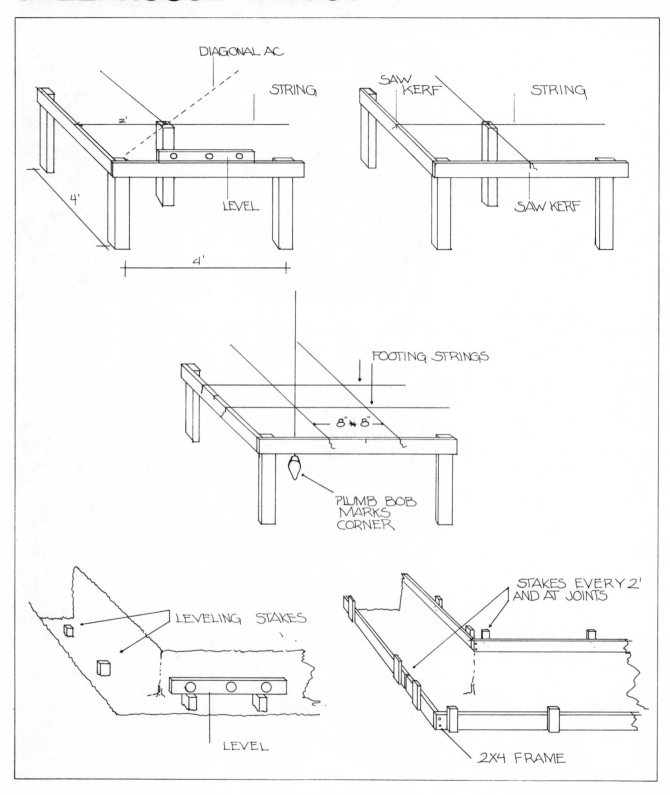

thicker foundations (footings) where there is excessive weight, such as around the building walls.

For a small area (5 X 10 feet) rent a power mixer and put in 1 part cement, 2 parts sand, and 2 parts gravel or aggregate. First put in the water, followed by the gravel and sand, finishing with the cement. Work quickly before drying sets in. Smooth the floor at one time.

For larger areas, buy ready-mixed concrete and have it delivered. A truck generally holds about 7 yards; the concrete is run from the chute of the truck directly into the site where you have the forms in place. (Having concrete pumped up a hill or into inaccessible places is more expensive.) Work fast, within a 30-minute period, or you will be charged overtime. Get two friends: one should guide the chute (or the truck driver might do this); you and the other friend should get the mix in place with floats and trowels. If concrete starts to set before you have finished the pour, you are in trouble, so keep working fast. As the concrete pours, poke sticks into the footings to be sure concrete gets to all voids in the trenches.

Screeding is distributing the concrete at a uniform level in the form area and is done with a screed board (a 2 X 4 nailed to a 1 X 2 handle). Wear rubber boots and push and bull the board to evenly distribute the concrete. Now, if you want to, tamp down the concrete. Run an expanded metal screen over the concrete to level the slab and bring water, sand, and cement to the surface. Use a 2 X 6 wooden board with a handle (a float) to further level

the concrete. Work the level *lightly* over large areas while the concrete is still wet; do not dig it in. Be sure the handle is long enough to reach the middle of the area of the slab from the outer edge. Use the float again when the concrete is somewhat set or looks sugary, and work in wide sweeps to level the slab.

Steel troweling, the final step, seals and waterproofs the slab and gets rid of minor defects. When the concrete has set, remove the forms. For a few days, especially if the weather is hot, cover the area with plastic or burlap and keep it sprinkled so it cures slowly; slow curing gives you a strong floor.

BRICK

Concrete is an excellent flooring material, but brick too has its merits; it is always handsome, easy to install, and weathers beautifully with time. Like concrete, it resists stain. Brick costs more than concrete.

The best brick for the greenhouse floor is smooth-surfaced or rough-textured common brick. Use hard-burned rather than green brick; use dark red brick rather than salmon, which indicates an underburned process and less durability. Keep the brick damp but not wet when laying it.

Brick can be laid on a sand base, but it is better to install it

A concrete slab floor was the first step in building this greenhouse. Concrete makes a durable floor that lasts for years. *(Photo by author).*

on a concrete slab with mortar. Use a thin mortar for laying the brick, with a heavier cement and grout in the interstices. (Dark-colored cement for grouting gives a more dramatic effect.) If you have to cut a brick, use a cold chisel and a brick hammer for making irregular cuts and trimming. Cut a groove along one side of the brick with the chisel or hammer, and then give it a final severing blow. Cut the brick on a solid level surface, such as a piece of wood. Smooth uneven edges by rubbing them with another brick.

CINDERS, GRAVEL

Cinders or gravel can be used for an inexpensive greenhouse floor; water evaporates slowly on these materials to provide good humidity for plants. For lightweight structures such as A frames and plastic covered designs on footings or piers, the cinder or gravel floor is excellent.

To install such a floor, dig down 4 to 6 inches and level the area. Insert gravel, rake it in place and put in more gravel until it is flush with the excavation.

Many times earth floors are used in greenhouses but they do get muddy so it is wise to put down some cinders or gravel over the earth.

WOOD FLOORS

Somewhat like decking, redwood floors can be used in greenhouses in temperate climates. The flooring is put in place with spaces between the boards so excess water can escape—of course, drafts and cold air can also enter through these spaces. Yet the redwood floor is handsome and as mentioned if climate will allow it do give it some consideration. Precast concrete piers are usually used as footings for wood floor greenhouses.

4 Greenhouse Design

Because the greenhouse is essentially for plants, you want a structure that admits ample light. But too much light can harm plants. An all-glass greenhouse is not necessary; most plants will grow beautifully under a roof that allows 30 percent natural light (this roof can be pitched, hipped, skylighted, domes, and so on). Let your imagination soar and get away from the stereotyped greenhouse.

The lean-to, or L or U-shaped, and court or atrium greenhouses are the most popular designs, but there are other types of places for plants. The A frame, the lath house, the square greenhouse, and so on are much cheaper to build, and they are easy to construct in, say, a weekend.

All of the above are types of greenhouse construction but you should also consider whether the greenhouse will be one with solar additions (panels) or an underground unit (to conserve heat), or a dome structure. Or if you do not have the space, a window greenhouse might be in order.

Lean-To Greenhouse

The attached lean-to greenhouse uses one wall of the house, thus saving you the construction of a fourth wall. This house wall also conducts some heat to the lean-to. If some artificial heat is needed in the lean-to, a duct from the house can be extended inexpensively into the pit. The lean-to also makes it convenient for you to get to your plants, even in inclement weather, because it adjoins the house—the garden is thus only a few steps away. However, because it is part of the house, the lean-to has to be always ship-shape since it is usually in view.

Also, because the lean-to is actually part of the house, its design should match (more or less) the design of the home so that the greenhouse indeed looks like it belongs rather than appearing like an afterthought. For example, a rustic house should have a rustic-looking lean-to, with heavy beams and thatched walls. If your house is more modern in design, the lean-to should have clean, simple lines, with a finished redwood or aluminum frame. Use a structural element of the house, say a post or moldings, in the lean-to to tie together the house and greenhouse and thus create a pleasing appearance.

The lean-to greenhouse has to have doors that enter to the house; the doors can be aluminum sliding ones (sold at home-supply stores or any good hardware store) or be the more conventional wooden ones (sold at lumber yards). Door openings should be at least 3 feet wide, with 6-inch thick wooden doors or 3-inch wide sliding doors; narrow doors make the lean-to look too confined. Doors must be properly fitted, and install weather stripping around the doors to prevent air leakage.

The floor of the lean-to should be water-resistant; use concrete or brick, but not wood. The joint where the roof of the lean-to is attached to the house wall must be prepared carefully so leaks do not develop. Remove the siding on the house, insert metal

ATTACHED GREENHOUSE

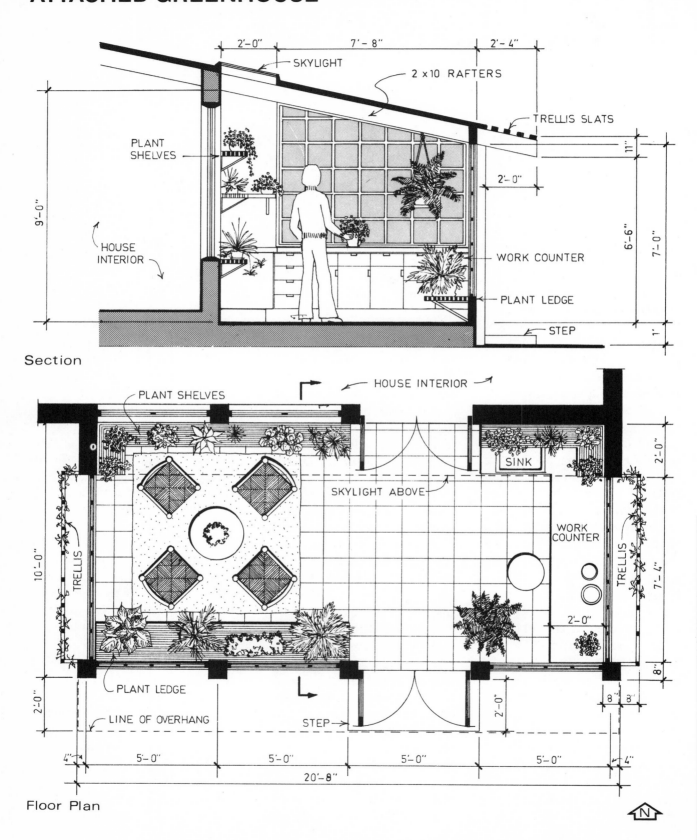

Section

Floor Plan

ATTACHED GREENHOUSE

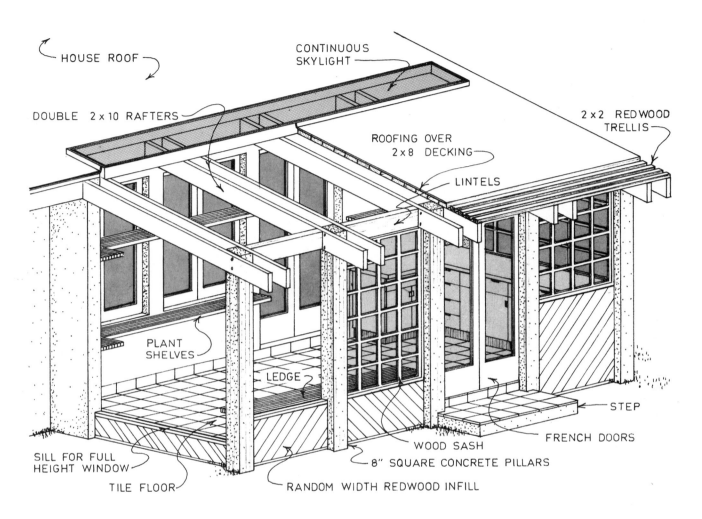

HOUSE ROOF

CONTINUOUS SKYLIGHT

DOUBLE 2 x 10 RAFTERS

2 x 2 REDWOOD TRELLIS

ROOFING OVER 2 x 8 DECKING

LINTELS

PLANT SHELVES

LEDGE

SILL FOR FULL HEIGHT WINDOW

TILE FLOOR

RANDOM WIDTH REDWOOD INFILL

8" SQUARE CONCRETE PILLARS

WOOD SASH

FRENCH DOORS

STEP

ROOF
CONTINUATION OF HOUSE ROOF, DOUBLE 2 x 10 RAFTERS BOLTED TO PILLARS, 2 x 8 DECKING W/ ROOFING ABOVE, 2 x 2 REDWOOD SLAT TRELLIS AT OVERHANG

SKYLIGHT
2' WIDE CONTINUOUS WIRE GLASS SKYLIGHT AT LINE OF HOUSE WALL, WOOD FRAMED

STRUCTURE
8" SQUARE REINFORCED CONCRETE PILLARS, 4 x 8 LINTELS ABOVE DOORS & WINDOWS, WOOD FRAME WALLS BELOW, W/ RANDOM WIDTH, DIAGONAL REDWOOD SIDING, WALLS ADJACENT TO HOUSE ARE A CONTINUATION OF THE HOUSE STRUCTURE

FLOOR & STEP
REINFORCED CONCRETE, INCLUDING FOOTINGS, WALL BASE & FLOOR TILED

WINDOWS
VARYING HEIGHTS, WOOD FRAMED W/OPERABLE WOOD SASH

DOORS
WOOD FRAMED DOUBLE FRENCH DOORS, ALSO INTO HOUSE INTERIOR

WORK COUNTER
PLYWOOD CABINETS, W/PLASTIC LAMINATE COUNTERTOP & STAINLESS STEEL SINK

PLANT SHELVES & LEDGE
1 x 2 REDWOOD SLATS ON STEEL BRACKETS, PLANT LEDGE ATTACHED TO WINDOW SILL

NOTE:
FOR SUMMER SOLAR PROTECTION ON EAST & WEST SIDES, TRAIN DECIDUOUS VINES ON RED-WOOD TRELLISES - ATTACH 1' AWAY FROM SIDE WINDOWS

CONVERTING A PORCH

Interior View

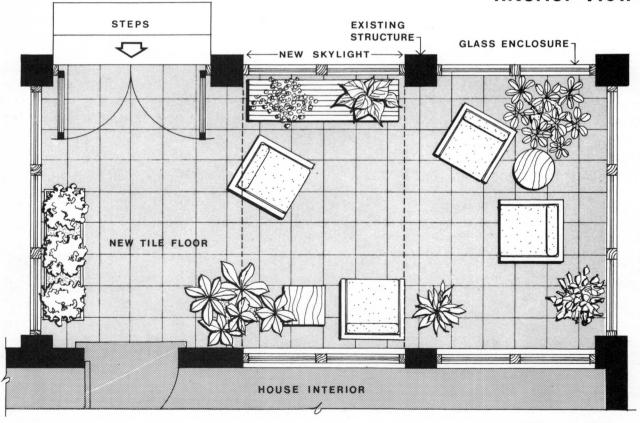

STEPS

EXISTING STRUCTURE

NEW SKYLIGHT

GLASS ENCLOSURE

NEW TILE FLOOR

HOUSE INTERIOR

Floor Plan

flashing to avoid leaks, and then replace the siding. I strongly recommend hiring a professional to do this work.

The roof of the lean-to should be either partially glass or have glass domes. For the average 16 X 20 greenhouse allow four 37- X 37-inch domes; for glass, allow 30 percent of the total square footage of the roof. For example, if you are using glass, and you have 320 square feet of roofing, 96 square feet of that roofing will be glass. You can also install a glass skylight, which is expensive, or use 1/4-inch plexiglass, which is easy to install and work with, comes in sheets you can cut yourself, and of course will not break.

CONVERTED PORCH

By using the lean-to principle, many people have successfully converted porches and patios into splendid greenhouses. The floor is generally existing—for a patio, usually concrete or brick; if a porch, wood or sometimes concrete. The construction is relatively easy, as for a lean-to.

Use post and beam construction and sloped roofs; the slope allows water to drain off. The roof may be tar and gravel with plastic domes or metal skylights. There are a variety of designs you can use; it all depends on your budget and imagination.

COURT (ATRIUM)

This style is more commonly called an atrium—an open-to-the sky area in the center of the house. Once roofed over it can become a charming greenhouse, an actual part of the home, and a definite asset because it is visible from most rooms and thus

presents a very pleasant view. The atrium greenhouse should always be in scale with the house.

Because the house walls are used as the basis for the court greenhouse, all you have to do is enclose the ceiling. Use glass skylights, or domes, or try translucent acrylic sheets of corrugated plastic on a wood frame.

L- OR U-SHAPED GREENHOUSE

This design offers the home owner many advantages because it means building only one or two walls and using house walls as the other supporting members of the greenhouse. Also, the addition of only one or two walls and a roof add space to the main

house and make it appear visually larger. Such a structure is shaded by the house from wind and, in some cases, hot sun.

The L or U shape can be as narrow as 6 feet and still lend a pleasing area that is in scale with most averaged-sized homes. It provides two areas of greenery: one as a display and one side as a working greenhouse. Also, the wraparound effect of such an enclosure can enhance the appearance of the house.

The construction of these greenhouses is even simpler than for the lean-to. It follows the same rules but requires less work and materials. The L or U shaped greenhouse is indeed a perfect way to add a place for plants to the home.

Inside a lean-to greenhouse you can see the basic construction using the house wall as one wall and a dome to admit natural light. Lean-to construction is relatively simple and porches or patios as well can be converted to a greenhouse. *(Photo by Clark Photo Graphics).*

L-SHAPED GREENHOUSE

HOUSE INTERIOR

dn

skylight over

6'

8'

a

Floor Plan

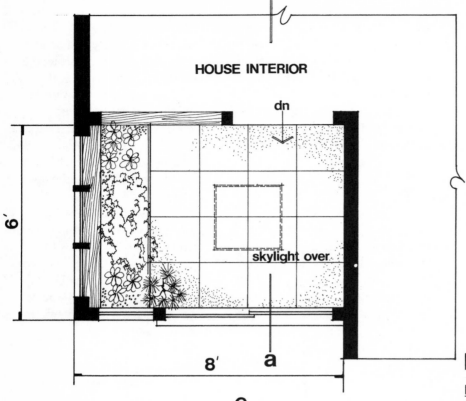

C

B

5

13

9

6

A

1'6"

10

8

7

11

7'0"

1

12

2 3 4

Section a

Materials

FOUNDATIONS
1. REINFORCED CONCRETE

FLOOR
2. CONCRETE
3. VAPOR BARRIER
4. GRAVEL

STRUCTURE
5. BEAMS 7-2×8s at 8'
6. HEADER 2-2×10s at 8'
7. POST 1-4×4 at 7'
8. MULLIONS 3-2×6s at 5'

WINDOW WALL
9. SKYLIGHT
10. GLASS
11. SLIDING GLASS DOOR 7'0"H × 5'0"W

CABINETS
12. PLYWOOD - 12 sq. ft.

ROOF
13. TAR & GRAVEL

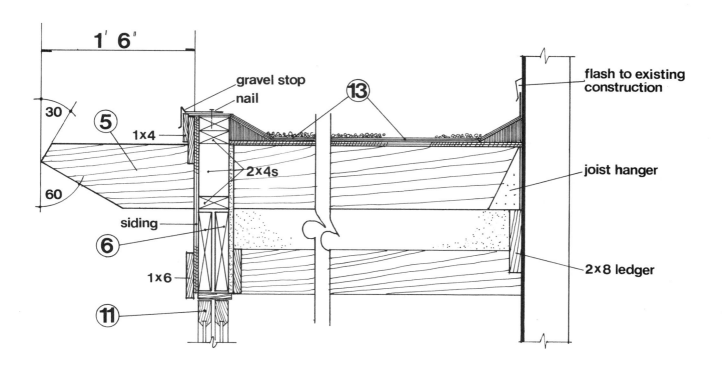

A
Details

B

Labels in image A: 1' 6", gravel stop, nail, 13, 30, 5, 1x4, 2x4s, 60, siding, 6, 1x6, 11, flash to existing construction, joist hanger, 2×8 ledger

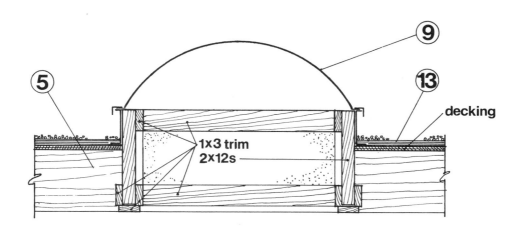

Detail C

Labels in image C: 9, 5, 13, decking, 1x3 trim, 2x12s

GALLERY GREENHOUSE

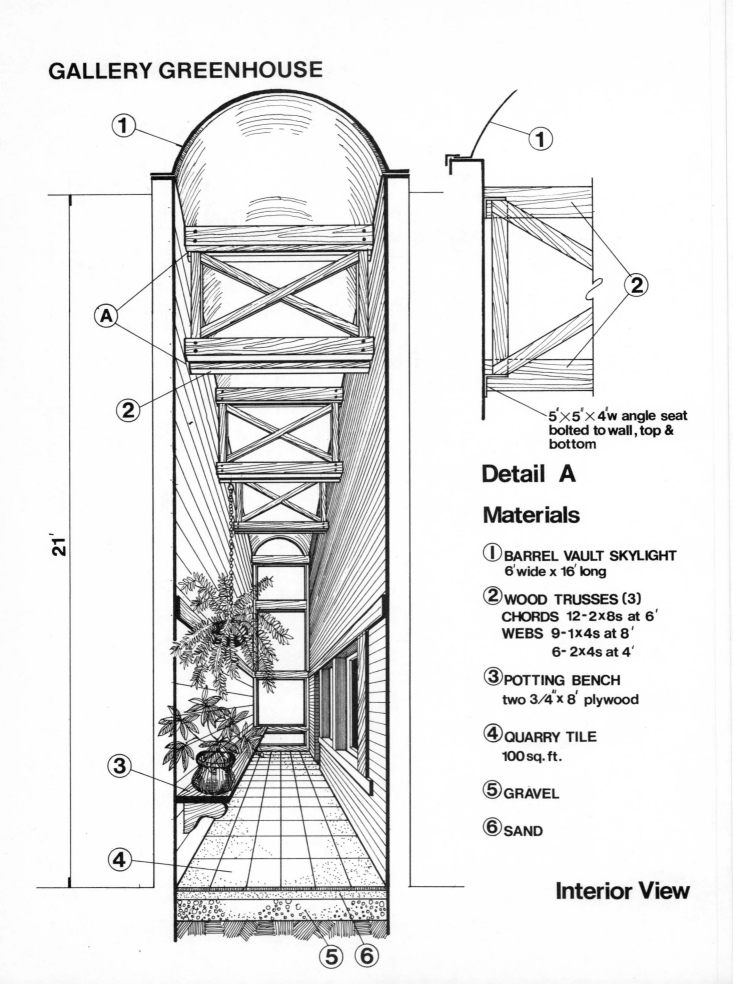

21′

5″×5″×4″w angle seat
bolted to wall, top &
bottom

Detail A

Materials

① BARREL VAULT SKYLIGHT
6′ wide x 16′ long

② WOOD TRUSSES (3)
CHORDS 12-2x8s at 6′
WEBS 9-1x4s at 8′
6-2x4s at 4′

③ POTTING BENCH
two 3/4″ x 8′ plywood

④ QUARRY TILE
100 sq. ft.

⑤ GRAVEL

⑥ SAND

Interior View

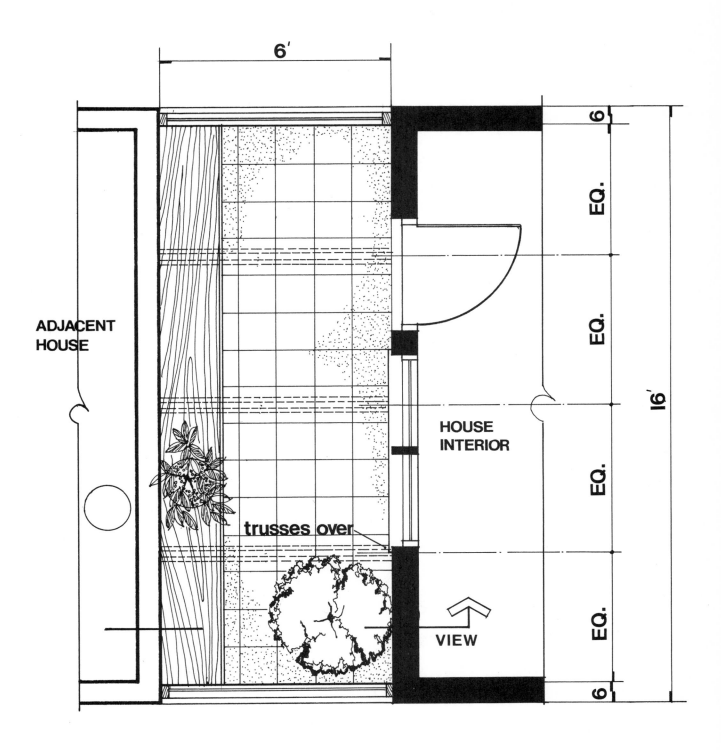

6'

ADJACENT
HOUSE

trusses over

HOUSE
INTERIOR

VIEW

6

EQ.

EQ.

EQ.

EQ.

6

16'

Floor Plan

LOFT GREENHOUSE

FLOOR PLANS

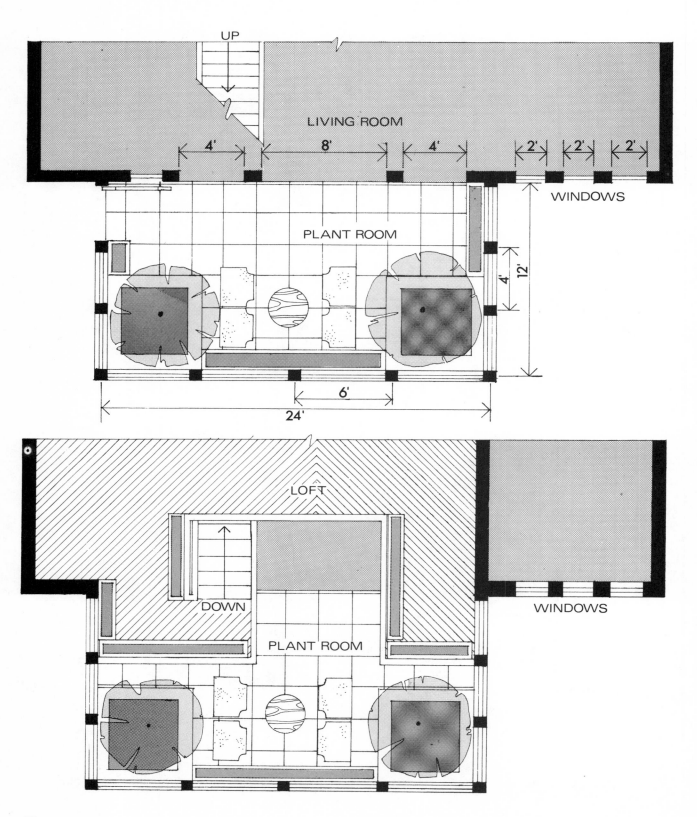

UP

LIVING ROOM

4' 8' 4' 2' 2' 2'

WINDOWS

PLANT ROOM

4' 12'

6'

24'

LOFT

DOWN

PLANT ROOM

WINDOWS

56

LOFT GREENHOUSE

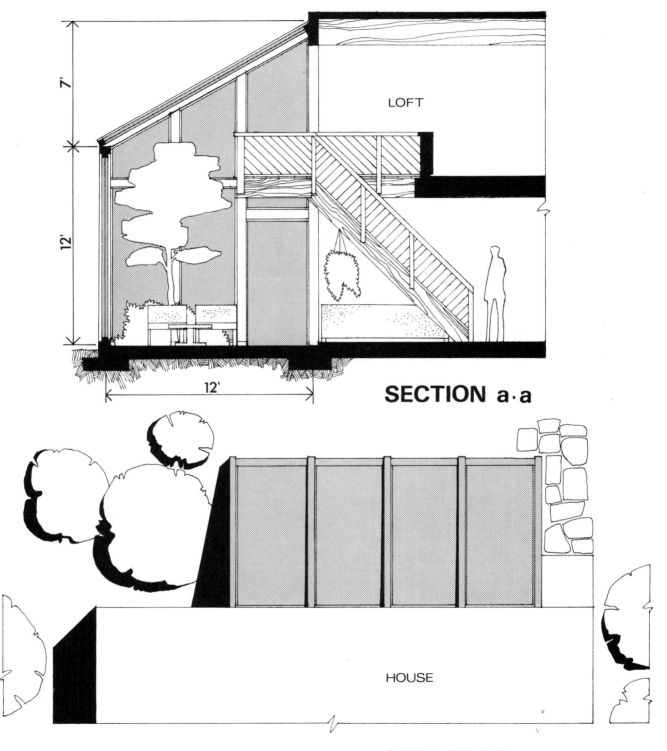

7'

LOFT

12'

12'

SECTION a·a

HOUSE

SITE PLAN

LOFT GREENHOUSE

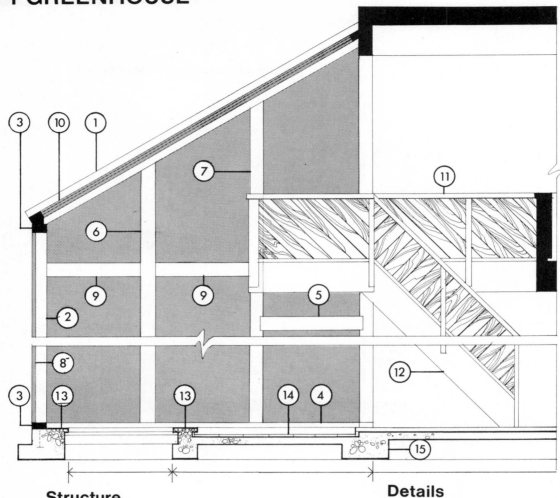

Structure

①RAFTERS 5-6X10sX15
②POSTS 5-6X6sX12
③PLATES 2-4X6X24

Windows

⑧WINDOW GLASS ON WOOD

Roof

⑩STEEL-FRAMED WIRED GLASS

Loft

⑪RAILING 2X6s&4s, REDWOOD
    PLANKING

Foundation   Floor

⑬EXPOSED AGGREGATE
⑭QUARRY TILE

Details

④2-4X6s X12
⑤HEADERS 4X8
⑥2-6X6sX15
⑦2-6X6sX17

⑨FRAMING 4X6

⑫LAMINATED WOOD

⑮REINFORCED CONCRETE

Materials

This atrium type greenhouse is elaborate and lovely and houses many, many plants as well as a seating area for people. It is a desirable addition to the home. *(Photo by Matthew Barr).*

GREENHOUSES IN THE AIR

Greenhouses on upper levels—garage roofs, on carports or rooms—are becoming popular because they are a separate entity and look dramatic. Most people think of the upper greenhouse as a lean-to but it can be a separate structure on a roof or on footings-and-posts (at building supply houses).

Make sure the design of the upstairs greenhouse is in character with the architecture of the adjoining building. Do not just add a box because it will always look just like a box! If it is on top of a room be sure the existing roof can take the extra weight (an architect can advise you). In such cases, flooring and drainage facilities must be near perfect so there is absolutely no leakage. A

second-floor greenhouse above a carport or on piers and footings, as mentioned, is thus more ideal because if some leakage does occur there is no harm.

The second floor greenhouse is generally of frame construction with a pitched roof. Posts can be 6 X 6, beams 6 X 8, and sills, 2 X 6. A suitable floor—concrete, decking, if weather permits—can be used. The roof can be partially wire glass or glass and wood; walls can be wood and glass also.

A Frame Greenhouse

The A frame looks good, is sensible because the triangle is one of the strongest geometric forms, can be put together in a

weekend, as mentioned, and can be converted into a permanent building if desired. Use redwood framing, with 2- X 4-foot rafters covered with flexible or rigid plastic. Dig two parallel trenches 12 inches deep and 12 inches wide. Nail four 2 X 12 rafters to a 1 X 10 ridge, and then raise the frame, supporting it by temporarily bracing it in the ground. Now nail the other rafters to the ridge, and fashion bridging between the rafters. Put the 2 X 4 and 2 X 2 cross braces in place between opposite rafters. At one end put in a frame for the door, and allow space for ventilating fans in two areas.

For the footing, pour a mixture of 1 part cement, 3 parts gravel, and 2 parts sand into the trench around the rafters. Do not

This steel and fiberglas greenhouse also uses the arch design and comes in three lengths. It is a very functional durable unit and is manufactured by Environmental Dynamics Company.

remove the braces until the concrete has thoroughly set. Next, saw cut fiberglas panels to fit the wooden frame; nail them to the frame, allowing one corrugation overlap between them. If you use flat material, allow a 2-inch overlap. To weatherproof the ceiling, apply mastic between the panels before nailing the panels in place (use aluminum nails, which do not rust).

The floor can be gravel, soil, or bricks laid in sand. For a gravel floor, dig down 4 to 6 inches, and then level the area. Rake gravel into place, and add more gravel until the floor is level with the excavation. Since the A frame is ideal for tall plants, hang plants from rafters (use wire or chain), place more plants on a bench along one wall of the A frame, and display floor specimen plants along the opposite wall.

ARCHED GREENHOUSE

The shape of this rather clean, neat greenhouse is conducive to growing many plants, tall and small. There is ample length and height, and the round lines are more in keeping with the human shape. It is strong, and new building materials make the arched greenhouse very feasible for the amateur carpenter.

You can also buy a fine prefabricated arch shape greenhouse make of kiln dried heart redwood glazed in fiberglas. The unit lacks the handcrafted look but it is certainly fine for plants and as mentioned previously you can add your own personal touches to give it some charm.

Whether you make your own arch greenhouse with I-beams or buy a prefab, remember that these are totally enclosed structures and fans will be necessary

to ensure fresh air circulation. These can be built into end walls. A portable space heater can be used for heating. This is a totally utilitarian structure, fine for plants and not costly. Again, I must say its appearance is somewhat alien to the natural scene but certainly not objectionable, and such a structure properly built can last a very long time.

LATH HOUSE

Too often this structure is of haphazard design and unattractive. Yet with some planning it can be a desirable functional feature in the landscape. It can be made of open slats to create a pleasing design or trellis work, which is indeed handsome. The lath house reduces the intensity of the sun, providing coolness within. The alternating sun and shade provides almost ideal conditions for plants.

The size and shape of the enclosure is determined by the site; a good size is 10 X 12 feet. The width of a single lath is generally the best space for maximum sun control, but a trellis ceiling (laths crossing) is acceptable too and more handsome. Construct the house with a sloping roof so rain runs down the laths and plants are protected from dripping water.

Because this is a lightweight structure, footings can be commercial precast concrete piers. Use 2 X 4 redwood for the vertical members, spaced about 4 feet apart; for roof construction use 2 X 4 beams. The lath house can be used without a covering as a temporary shelter, finished with fiberglas, or glazed with lightweight acrylic for a permanent place.

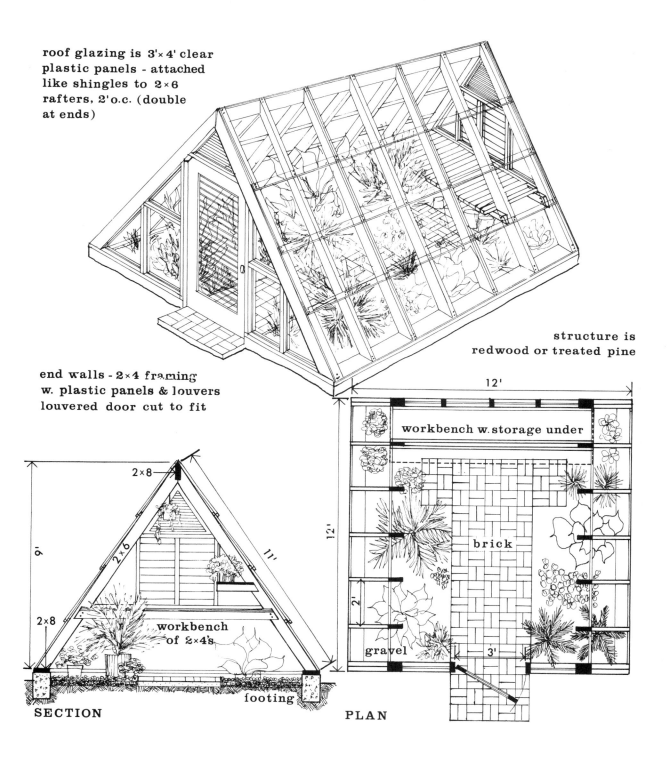

roof glazing is 3'×4' clear plastic panels - attached like shingles to 2×6 rafters, 2'o.c. (double at ends)

structure is redwood or treated pine

end walls - 2×4 framing w. plastic panels & louvers louvered door cut to fit

2×8

2×6

9'

11'

2×8

workbench of 2×4's

footing

SECTION

12'

workbench w. storage under

12'

brick

2'

gravel

3'

PLAN

ROOF-TOP GREENHOUSE

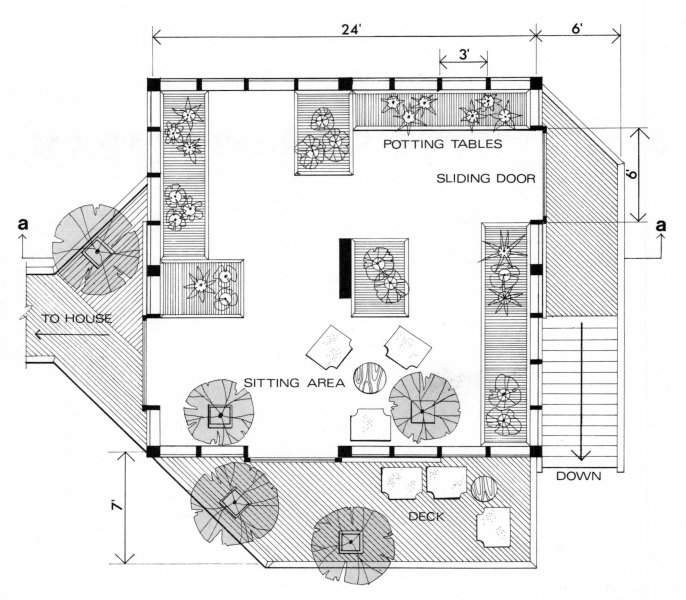

24'

6'

3'

POTTING TABLES

SLIDING DOOR

6'

a

a

TO HOUSE

SITTING AREA

DOWN

7'

DECK

Floor Plan

ROOF-TOP GREENHOUSE

SECTION a-a

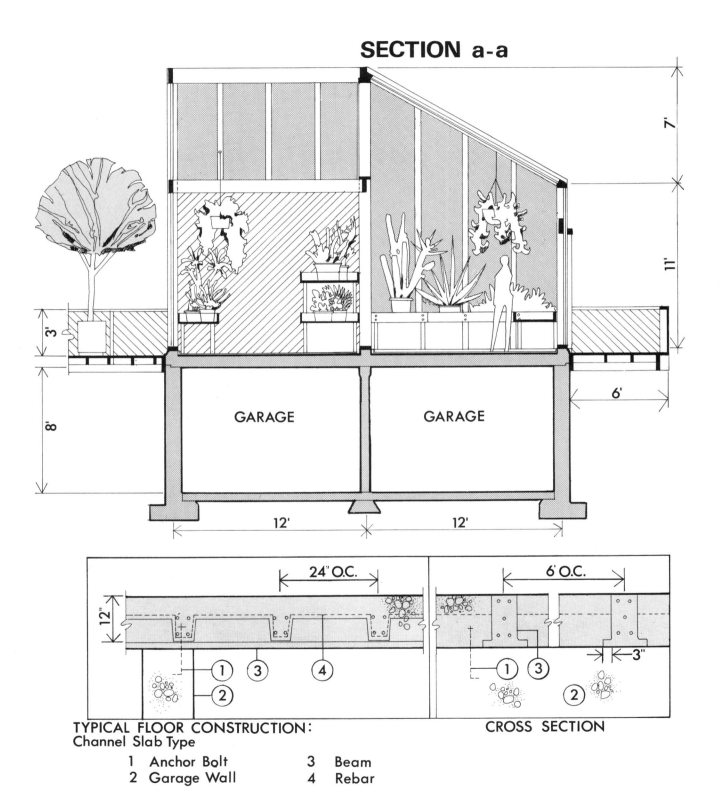

7'

11'

3'

8'

6'

GARAGE

GARAGE

12'

12'

24" O.C.

6' O.C.

12"

3"

① ③ ④

②

① ③

②

TYPICAL FLOOR CONSTRUCTION:
Channel Slab Type

CROSS SECTION

1 Anchor Bolt   3 Beam
2 Garage Wall   4 Rebar

LOW COST GREENHOUSE

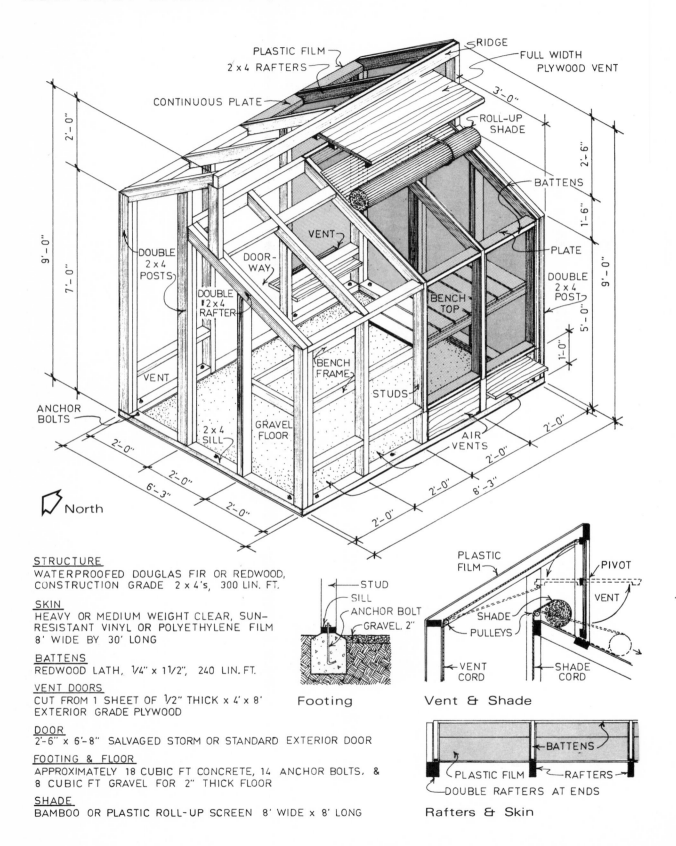

PLASTIC FILM
2 x 4 RAFTERS

RIDGE

FULL WIDTH
PLYWOOD VENT

CONTINUOUS PLATE

3'-0"

ROLL-UP
SHADE

2'-6"

BATTENS

1'-6"

2'-0"

VENT

DOUBLE
2 x 4
POSTS

DOOR-
WAY

9'-0"

7'-0"

DOUBLE
2 x 4
RAFTER

PLATE

DOUBLE
2 x 4
POST

9'-0"

BENCH
TOP

5'-0"

VENT

BENCH
FRAME

STUDS

1'-0"

ANCHOR
BOLTS

GRAVEL
FLOOR

AIR
VENTS

2'-0"

2'-0"

2'-0"

2'-0"

2'-0"

2'-0"

6'-3"

2'-0"

8'-3"

2'-0"

North

STRUCTURE
WATERPROOFED DOUGLAS FIR OR REDWOOD,
CONSTRUCTION GRADE 2 x 4's, 300 LIN. FT.

SKIN
HEAVY OR MEDIUM WEIGHT CLEAR, SUN-
RESISTANT VINYL OR POLYETHYLENE FILM
8' WIDE BY 30' LONG

BATTENS
REDWOOD LATH, 1/4" x 1 1/2", 240 LIN. FT.

VENT DOORS
CUT FROM 1 SHEET OF 1/2" THICK x 4' x 8'
EXTERIOR GRADE PLYWOOD

DOOR
2'-6" x 6'-8" SALVAGED STORM OR STANDARD EXTERIOR DOOR

FOOTING & FLOOR
APPROXIMATELY 18 CUBIC FT CONCRETE, 14 ANCHOR BOLTS, &
8 CUBIC FT GRAVEL FOR 2" THICK FLOOR

SHADE
BAMBOO OR PLASTIC ROLL-UP SCREEN 8' WIDE x 8' LONG

STUD
SILL
ANCHOR BOLT
GRAVEL, 2"

Footing

PLASTIC
FILM

PIVOT

VENT

SHADE
PULLEYS

VENT
CORD

SHADE
CORD

Vent & Shade

BATTENS

PLASTIC FILM

RAFTERS

DOUBLE RAFTERS AT ENDS

Rafters & Skin

Arched greenhouse design affords ample room for plants, is easy to build and inexpensive. This one is glazed with corrugated fiberglas and comes from the Gothic Arch Greenhouse Company as a prefabricated kit.

This steel and fiberglas greenhouse also uses the arch design and comes in three lengths. It is a very functional durable unit and is manufactured by Environmental Dynamics Company.

ARCHED GREENHOUSE

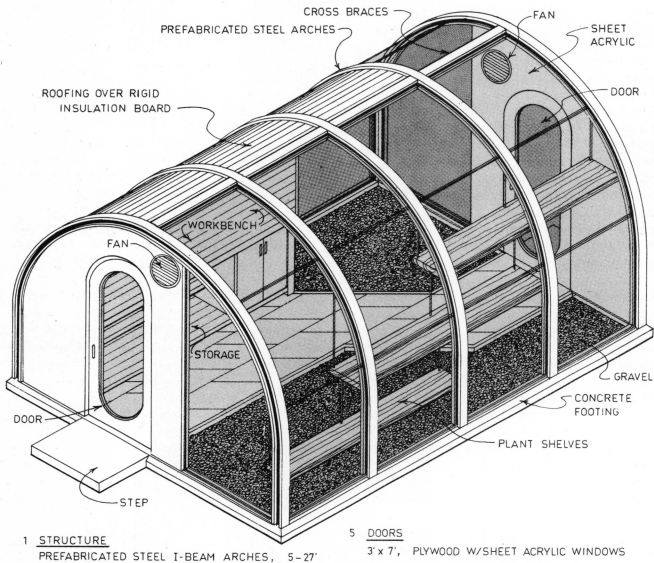

CROSS BRACES

PREFABRICATED STEEL ARCHES

FAN

SHEET ACRYLIC

ROOFING OVER RIGID INSULATION BOARD

DOOR

WORKBENCH

FAN

STORAGE

GRAVEL

CONCRETE FOOTING

DOOR

PLANT SHELVES

STEP

1 <u>STRUCTURE</u>

PREFABRICATED STEEL I-BEAM ARCHES, 5 – 27' LONG x 4" SQ., 6' RADIUS SEMICIRCLE, SET INTO CONCRETE FOOTING   I-BEAM BRACES AT TOP

2 <u>OPAQUE ROOF & WALLS</u>

3" THICK RIGID INSULATION BOARD, WATERPROOFED, ROOFING OVER ARCHED SURFACES

3 <u>TRANSPARENT ROOF & WALLS</u>

1/8" SHEET ACRYLIC PLASTIC IN ALUMINUM FRAMES

4 <u>FLOOR</u>

CONCRETE TILES IN REDWOOD FRAMING & GRAVEL OVER SOIL, CONCRETE STEPS AT DOORS

5 <u>DOORS</u>

3' x 7', PLYWOOD W/SHEET ACRYLIC WINDOWS

6 <u>WORK/STORAGE UNIT</u>

REDWOOD WORKBENCH & SHELVES, REDWOOD PLYWOOD STORAGE CABINET

7 <u>PLANT SHELVES</u>

REDWOOD, 8' LONG, VARYING WIDTHS, SUSPENDED BY STEEL RODS FROM ARCHES

NOTE:

SPACE IS VENTED BY FANS BUILT INTO END WALLS, & HEATED WITH A PORTABLE SPACE HEATER

ARCHED GREENHOUSE

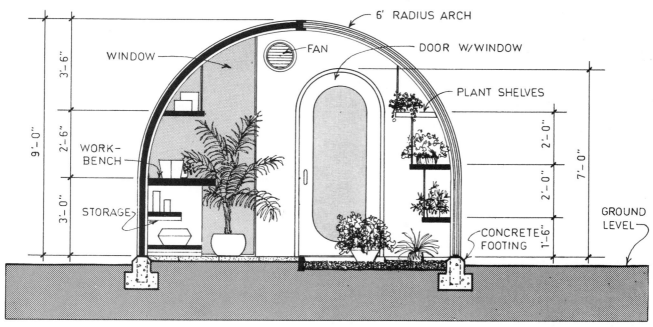

6' RADIUS ARCH

WINDOW

FAN

DOOR W/WINDOW

PLANT SHELVES

WORK-BENCH

STORAGE

3'-6"

2'-6"

3'-0"

9'-0"

2'-0"

2'-0"

2'-0"

1'-6"

7'-0"

CONCRETE FOOTING

GROUND LEVEL

Section

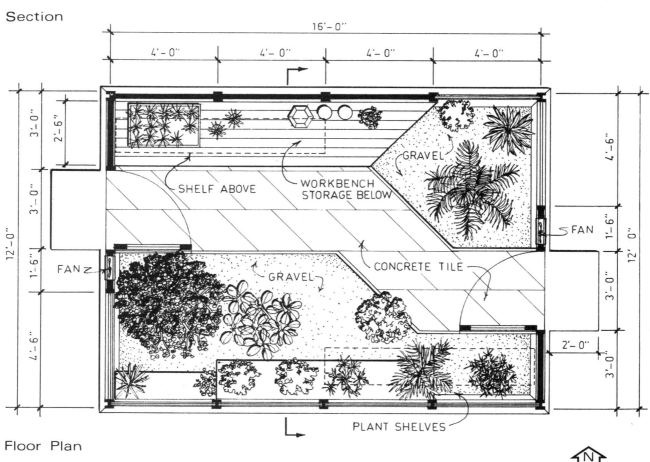

16'-0"

4'-0"

4'-0"

4'-0"

4'-0"

3'-0"

2'-6"

3'-0"

1'-6"

4'-6"

12'-0"

SHELF ABOVE

WORKBENCH STORAGE BELOW

GRAVEL

FAN

FAN

GRAVEL

CONCRETE TILE

4'-6"

1'-6"

3'-0"

2'-0"

3'-0"

12'-0"

PLANT SHELVES

Floor Plan

N

LATH GREENHOUSE

all lumber is redwood or
treated pine

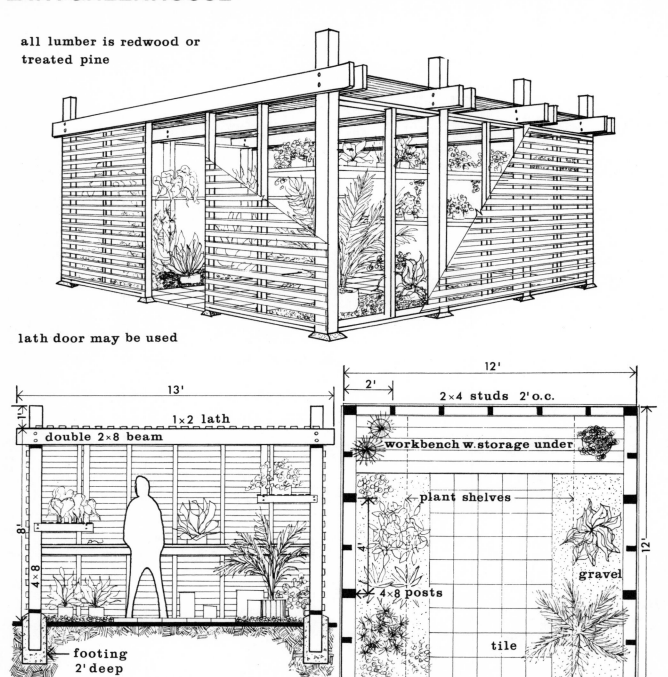

lath door may be used

SECTION

13'

1"

1×2 lath

double 2×8 beam

8'

4×8

footing
2' deep

PLAN

12'

2'

2×4 studs 2' o.c.

workbench w. storage under

plant shelves

4'

4×8 posts

gravel

tile

12'

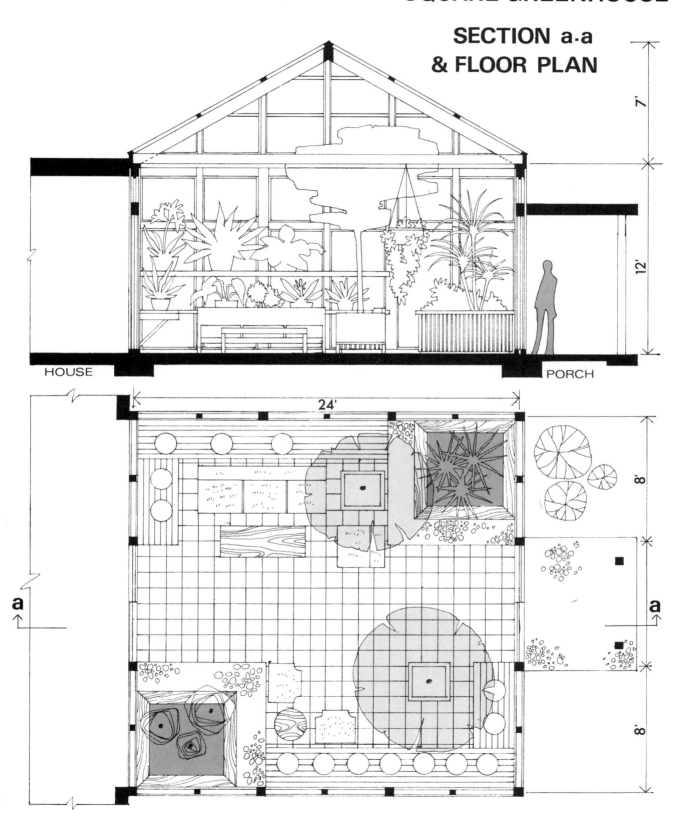

SQUARE GREENHOUSE

SECTION a·a
& FLOOR PLAN

7'

12'

HOUSE

PORCH

24'

8'

8'

a

a

SQUARE GREENHOUSE

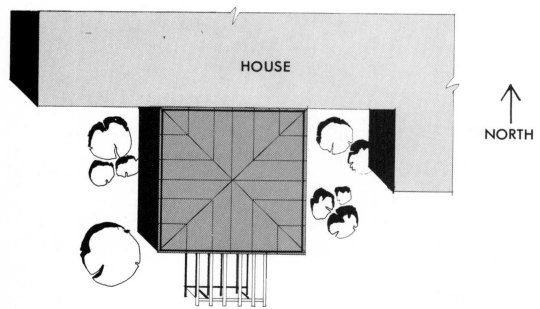

HOUSE

↑
NORTH

SITE PLAN

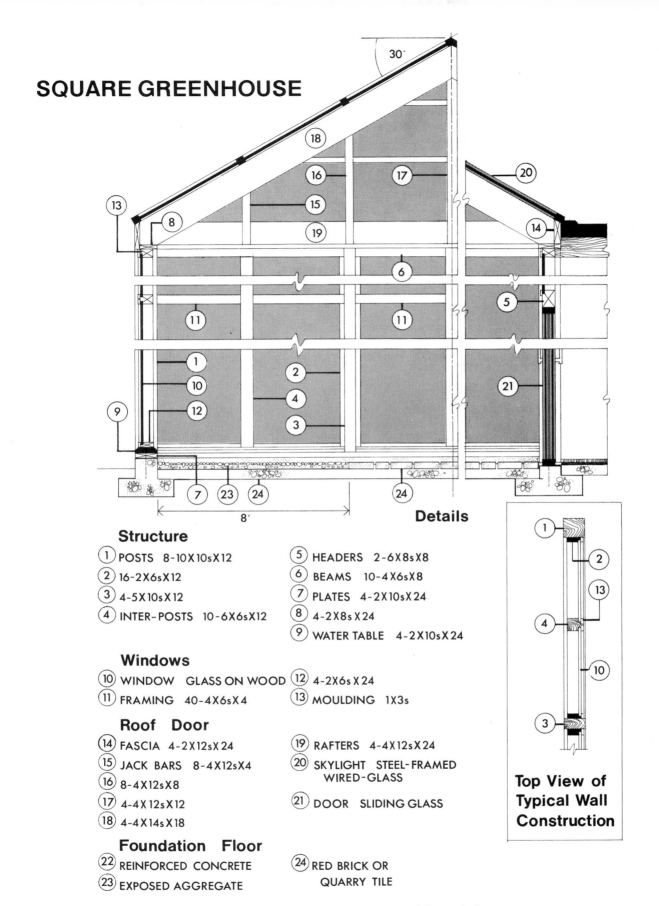

SQUARE GREENHOUSE

30°

Details

Structure

1. POSTS 8-10X10sX12
2. 16-2X6sX12
3. 4-5X10sX12
4. INTER-POSTS 10-6X6sX12
5. HEADERS 2-6X8sX8
6. BEAMS 10-4X6sX8
7. PLATES 4-2X10sX24
8. 4-2X8sX24
9. WATER TABLE 4-2X10sX24

Windows

10. WINDOW GLASS ON WOOD
11. FRAMING 40-4X6sX4
12. 4-2X6sX24
13. MOULDING 1X3s

Roof Door

14. FASCIA 4-2X12sX24
15. JACK BARS 8-4X12sX4
16. 8-4X12sX8
17. 4-4X12sX12
18. 4-4X14sX18
19. RAFTERS 4-4X12sX24
20. SKYLIGHT STEEL-FRAMED WIRED-GLASS
21. DOOR SLIDING GLASS

Foundation Floor

22. REINFORCED CONCRETE
23. EXPOSED AGGREGATE
24. RED BRICK OR QUARRY TILE

8′

Materials

Top View of Typical Wall Construction

This lath house was built for less than $50 and is a fine temporary place for plants. Again, it can always be glazed later with suitable weathertight materials. *(Photo by Clark Photo Graphics).*

A simple rectangular greenhouse is a sanctuary for plants—and you too. Of wood, plastic, and glass, this is a detached unit in a yard. *(Photo by Matthew Barr).*

SQUARE OR RECTANGULAR GREENHOUSE

This detached and inexpensive structure is easy to build in a weekend. Use corrugated or flat, rigid fiberglas sheets throughout and 2 X 4s with 2 X 6 rafters for framing. A sliding glass door works fine for an entrance. Select any color fiberglas you like, but the more neutral shades blend better with the landscape than very bright colors.

Use post and beam construction, with a redwood skeleton. Nail the fiberglas sheets in place with overlapping joints of 2 inches; use a plastic mastic between joints to ensure weatherproofing. Allow for an overhang; it makes the building look better. Pitch the roof slightly so water runs off. Because no windows are involved (there is no need for them), provide ventilation (fans and louvers).

For the floor, dig out 4 inches of soil, level the area of debris, and insert a bed of gravel. This material will of course have to be replaced periodically, but it does supply good humidity in the greenhouse as water on it evaporates. The support for the greenhouse can be concrete piers at each corner because little weight is involved.

A variation of this kind of construction is shown in the drawing titled Low-Cost Greenhouse, where 2 X 4s are used almost exclusively throughout the structure—for rafters, posts and beams. The frame is then covered with polyethylene film for a very inexpensive yet good-looking and functional greenhouse.

Another kind of greenhouse you might consider for a small indoor area is a tubular plastic and acrylic covered minigreen-house with an arch shape. This is offered as a prefabricated kit and snaps together in fifteen minutes without a single nut, bolt, screw or tool required. It can occupy any space near a window in an office, home, or apartment, and can also be fitted with a clip-on "plant-lite". (See list of suppliers at end of book.)

5 Advantages Of A Greenhouse

In a greenhouse you can work with plants, enjoying nature firsthand. Your private Eden may be a place to grow cut flowers, sow seeds to get a head start on spring, or start vegetables (and really save money). Also, and this is a big plus, you can relieve the day's tensions by working with nature.

Growing Plants from Seed

The gardener who grows his plants from seed gets more than economic advantages: he can have the most recently introduced plants. I still remember having the first dwarf red impatiens in full bloom long before they were available to the public. Also, by growing from seed you can have all the old favorites that are getting lost in the modern-day shuffle. A friend gave me some seeds of a forgotten iris, today unavailable commercially. From the seeds I have grown these flowers and in turn given seeds to other friends; this is an excellent way of keeping a line of plants going. Finally, often the color of flower or variety of vegetable you want is not available at your local garden center, so growing plants from seed in your greenhouse gives you a choice of selection.

GETTING STARTED

You can buy seeds from suppliers or order from seed catalogs, everything from house plants to vegetables and herbs. Or you collect seeds from friends' plants or the roadside. After you have made your seed selections, get some seed starting mediums—vermiculite, sand, and so on—containers, and equipment. New growing mediums and containers are available at suppliers. Perlite is a good growing medium, and milled sphagnum moss represents a tremendous advance in seed-starting techniques. You can also use Jiffy peat pots or Poly-trays.

SEED CONTAINERS AND GROWING MEDIUMS

There are many containers for starting seeds, both professionally made and homemade. Suppliers carry "starting kits," pot, plant mixes, and so forth. Just what kind of container you use depends upon your taste. For years my favorites have been the packing boxes (flats) for window glass because they are an ideal size, not too large or too small, and they are free. Flats range in size from 12 X 18 to 24 X 30 inches, 3 or 4 inches deep, and have drainage space between the boards. Flats are still available from glass dealers in some cities, usually free.

Other free containers to sow seeds in include such household items as coffee cans, aluminum and glass baking dishes, plastic cheese containers, and the aluminum pans that frozen rolls come in. Any household item you use as a container must be at least 3 inches deep and have some drainage facilities (punch tiny holes in the bottom of pans). In aluminum and plastic containers the planting mix will dry out quickly, so water more frequently.

You can also use the standard clay pot for seed sowing. These excellent containers are inexpensive, always look neat, and hold enough moisture so that frequent watering is not necessary.

Ask for azalea pans—squatty pots—now available in several sizes.

The growing medium you choose for seeds depends on what you want to grow. However, most seeds germinate easily in vermiculite or a standard "starting mix" (at nurseries). I have found that a peat mix is good for cactus and succulents; standard vermiculite and milled sphagnum are very satisfactory for annuals and perennials; and for starting trees and shrubs I use equal parts of sphagnum and vermiculite. Good growing mediums are:

Milled sphagnum. This old-timer generally gives good results. Its disadvantage is that it has to be carefully watered to maintain an evenly moist bed.

Perlite. This is a light, clean, volcanic ash that does not absorb moisture readily, but it holds moisture within itself, providing a moist growing medium ideal for seeds. Mix in a little sterilized soil so seeds do not float to the top.

Vermiculite. Vermiculite is expanded mica that holds moisture a long time. It is sold under various trade names, and frequently it is packaged with added ingredients, which may or may not be a good idea (I have not tried it yet).

Many gardeners prefer a mixture of equal parts vermiculite, sphagnum, and perlite. Avoid packaged soil mixes because they are generally too heavy for successful seed sowing. But if nothing else is at hand, use it in combination with some sand.

CUT FLOWERS

When days are gray and your spirits are depressed, the best cure is to walk into your greenhouse and cut some flowers for indoor decoration. Growing blooms under glass is easy, convenient, and cheap with controlled conditions. For a continuous supply of flowers, place the plants directly in wooden benches filled with soil. Although carnations and chrysanthemums are always favorites for bench growing, snapdragons, asters, calendulas, and alyssum are also fine possibilities, and there are dozens more.

Prepare your soil bed with care; this and watering is almost all you have to do for splendid flowers. Fill the bench with a copius layer of drainage material—shards or pebbles. Now add a good potting soil; you want a rich soil to get plants to grow quickly. Next, put the seedlings in place. (The seedlings can be plants you started yourself from seed in the greenhouse or seedlings you bought from a nursery.) Do not water too much at first; keep the seedlings just barely moist. Keep the humidity at about 50 to 60 percent to encourage good growth. Try not to grow too many different kinds of plants at first. Try a few together, such as snapdragons and stock, the first year. The following year grow several kinds. In time you will gain actual know-how experience, and your home will have cut flowers year-round.

Because there are so many cut flowers for greenhouse growing, it is impossible to offer a comprehensive list. Here are some favorites to try:

Ageratum
Aster
Buddleia
Butterfly flower (Schizanthus)
Chrysanthemum
Delphinium
Marguerite
Marigold (Tagetes)
Nasturtium (Tropaeolum)
Pansy
Phlox (annual)
Snapdragon
Statice
Stock
Sweet pea
Zinnia

STARTING PLANTS FOR OUTDOORS

As mentioned, besides being economical, growing plants in a greenhouse is an excellent way to stock the garden. You know what you have, and there is a great reward in looking over your landscape and knowing these are your plants. Start the seeds as described earlier in this chapter.

The following plants are ideal for starting in a greenhouse and getting a head start on spring:

Ageratum houstonianum (flossflower)
Anchusa capensis
Antirrhinum majus (snapdragon)
Arctotis stoechadifolia grandis (African daisy)
Calendula officinalis (pot marigold)
Centaurea cyanus (cornflower)
Cleome spinosa (spiderflower)
Cobaea scandens (sup-and-saucer vine)
Cosmos bipinnatis
Dimorphotheca aurantiaca
Gaillardia pulchella (annual)
Godetia grandiflora
Gypsophila elegans (annual)

The advantages of your own greenhouse are many and one facet is starting your own plants from seed. What a saving! And what a satisfaction of growing your own. *(Photo by Matthew Barr).*

Seedlings grow under almost perfect conditions in a greenhouse and prosper to mature into healthy plants. There is a money saving here as well as the joy of working with living plants. *(Photo by Matthew Barr).*

Helichrysum bracteatum (strawflower)
Impatiens balsamina (balsam)
Linum grandiflorum
Lobelia erinus (annual)
Mathiola incana (stock)
Myosotis alpestris
Petunia hybrids
Phlox drummondii (annual phlox)
Reseda odorata (mignonette)
Salpiglossis sinuata (painted tongue)
Scabiosa atropurpurea (pincushion flower)
Tagetes erecta (African marigold)
T. patula (French marigold)
Thunbergia alata (black-eyed Susan)
Verbena hortensis (garden verbena)

Vegetables and Herbs

If you have the space, grow some vegetables and herbs in addition to plants. Your own vegetables are a fabulous bounty, especially during bleak winter days, and herbs for salads and stews—fresh from the greenhouse—are impossible to buy. It is not necessary to have a lot of vegetables, and space probably will prohibit it anyway, but a few carrots, beets, and tomatoes are always welcome.

The joys of vegetable growing far outweigh the care you have to give the plants. Most vegetables grown in greenhouses—tomatoes, radishes, carrots—need only a good lightweight, quick-draining soil and plenty of sun. Keep the plants well watered after the seedlings have been put in their permanent locations, and provide

In the main, this greenhouse is used for house plants and what fine specimens the plants are. Begonias and ferns, cacti and succulents, grace this homemade greenhouse. *(Photo by Matthew Barr).*

Geraniums are the occupants of this greenhouse with nasturtiums growing at the door. Quite a pleasant sight. *(Photo by Matthew Barr).*

All kinds of plants thrive in this greenhouse including tuberous begonias, bougan-villea, seedlings, and even cut flowers. *(Photo by Clark Photo Graphics).*

a buoyant humidity of about 50 percent.

Tomatoes can be grown in large tubs. In fact, there is now a tomato variety that was especially developed for container growing. Grow plants in 80F to a single stem and stake them for support or it will be impossible to handle them. Polinate blossoms by hand, or use a hormone-type tomato spray on the blossoms.

Bibb lettuce grows in the same temperature as tomatoes and needs only an even soil and some sun. Carrots and beets need cooler growing conditions, about 45 to 55F.

You can start herbs from seeds or buy them as seedlings at nurseries; you may not want too many at first. A few selected herbs such as basil, dill, sweet margoram, tarragon, and a few chives may be all you need for your cooking purposes. Most herbs do fine with plenty of sun and a minimum temperature of 50F. Use rich soil and provide near-perfect drainage. Provide adequate humidity and good air circulation, and mist the plants occasionally to keep them in tip-top condition.

Houseplants

Although it is true that house-plants are for the house, it is nice to have these plants decorating the greenhouse if there is space. And there they will really grow, putting on a fine display. Indeed, medium-sized plants grown in the greenhouse will decorate your home and save you much money. With ideal conditions, plants will grow rapidly, and soon be ready for indoor display.

If your houseplants, look a little wilted and need some help, move them to the greenhouse for a few months. The good humidity and light will help restore them to health and save you from replacing plants that may have perished in bad conditions indoors.

Most houseplants will adapt and thrive in greenhouse conditions, that is, temperatures of 68 to 80F by day and 10 degrees less at night. Some tropical plants require high humidity and temperatures and so may not succeed in the greenhouse, but these plants are the exception rather than the rule.

6 Greenhouse Conditions And Maintenance

Once you have built your greenhouse, you must consider such requirements as temperature, humidity, and ventilation. If the greenhouse is an all-glass, tightly enclosed room, these requirements are vital because glass is a poor conductor and greenhouses are invariably too hot in summer and too cold in winter. However, if you have avoided the all-glass unit, the problems of temperature, humidity, and ventilation are less stringent. Basically, conditions that approximate home conditions, that is, average temperatures of 70 to 80F during the day and some cooling at night, are fine. Humidity of 30 to 60 percent is ideal, along with year-round circulation of air, which plants need.

Humidity

There is no reason to be confused about humidity in relation to growing plants. Average humidity (30 to 50 percent) is fine for most plants. High humidity, which is often recom-

mended for plants by so-called experts, can do more harm than good in the winter because when coupled with dark days it can create a breeding ground for plant fungus and bacteria. Use an inexpensive hygrometer in the greenhouse to measure the moisture in the air. And remember that the more artificial heat you use in winter, the more moisture in the air will be necessary. On very hot days keep the humidity somewhat high. At night, humidity, like temperature, should be lower if you want good plant growth.

Usually, many plants growing together will create their own humidity, so expensive equipment (misters, foggers) is not necessary unless it is very hot. As long as you water routinely, there will be sufficient humidity in a room of plants to create good growth.

Temperature

Most plants do just fine with a temperature of 70 to 80F during the day and a 10- to 15-degree

drop at night. You can maintain this temperature range in your own greenhouse without elaborate equipment; only in winter will you need to adjust heat for those very cold nights (and a few very cold nights will not harm plants). What will harm plants are sudden changes in temperatures, but by carefully manipulating windows and doors you can gradually cool summer evening temperatures. On very hot days, even the home greenhouse of wood and glass can get too hot for plants. When doors and windows are open, the sun can push the inside temperature past 100F, which dessicates plants and causes them to lose moisture fast. Spray and mist plants with water to keep them cool. Be especially alert in prolonged heat spells because you can lose many plants in a short few days if you do not cool them by misting or by providing outside shade (see later section).

In winter, do not fret if the greenhouse is somewhat cool. It is far better to keep plants cool than too hot: they can recover from a chill but rarely from

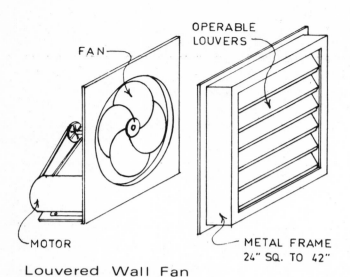

FAN

OPERABLE LOUVERS

MOTOR

METAL FRAME 24" SQ. TO 42"

Louvered Wall Fan

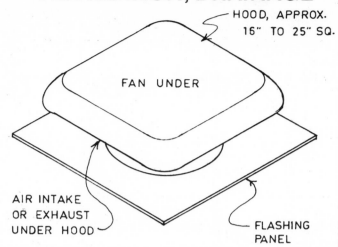

HOOD, APPROX. 16" TO 25" SQ.

FAN UNDER

AIR INTAKE OR EXHAUST UNDER HOOD

FLASHING PANEL

Roof Fan

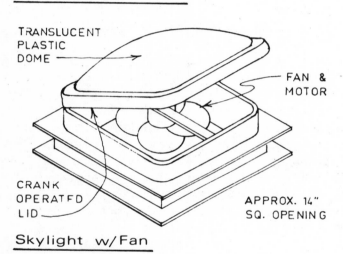

TRANSLUCENT PLASTIC DOME

FAN & MOTOR

CRANK OPERATED LID

APPROX. 14" SQ. OPENING

Skylight w/Fan

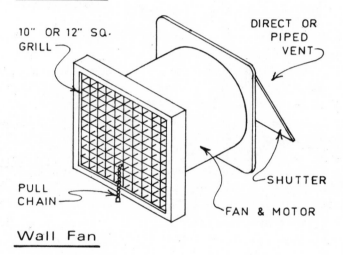

10" OR 12" SQ. GRILL

DIRECT OR PIPED VENT

PULL CHAIN

SHUTTER

FAN & MOTOR

Wall Fan

Ventilators

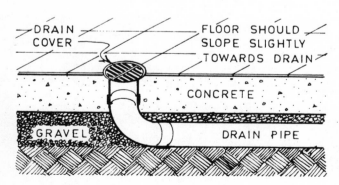

DRAIN COVER

FLOOR SHOULD SLOPE SLIGHTLY TOWARDS DRAIN

CONCRETE

GRAVEL

DRAIN PIPE

Solid Floor

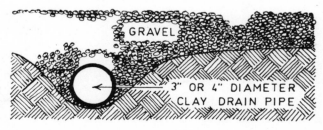

GROUND IS SLOPED TOWARDS CLAY PIPE IN TRENCH

GRAVEL

3" OR 4" DIAMETER CLAY DRAIN PIPE

Gravel Floor

dehydration. On very windy and cold days, the temperature in a greenhouse can drop faster than you think, so make sure sufficient heat is provided. Again, avoid drastic temperature changes in the greenhouse.

Ventilation

I have always considered ventilation in my greenhouse more important than humidity or temperature because a good circulation of air is essential for all plants. Good ventilation provides relief from the sun, helps control such disease problems as mildew, and assures good humidity. When I first started growing orchids, I was always concerned with humidity and tropical heat, but in a few years I discovered that the plants did not object to coolness; indeed, they grew better as long as there was adequate ventilation.

The atmosphere in the greenhouse should be bouyant and fresh, never stagnant or stale. If you observe nature, you will note that few plants grow in stagnant places. Take a clue from Mother Nature: keep ventilation at a maximum in your greenhouse. And even in winter be sure some air is entering the greenhouse. Rémember that hot air rises, so provide some window facilities at the top of the greenhouse. When windows or vents are open, warm air flows out to cool the greenhouse and provides fresh air for best growing conditions.

Shading

Direct summer sun can heat up a greenhouse considerably and

Every greenhouse should have a hygrometer (shown center in this picture) to measure the amount of moisture in the air. It saves a lot of guesswork. *(Photo by Matthew Barr).*

Temperature and hygrometer controls are located on the post in this place for plants. *(Photo by Matthew Barr).*

Ventilation is of prime importance in a greenhouse and here a fan is used. This in combination with the door provides ample circulation of air on very hot days. *(Photo by Matthew Barr).*

wreak havoc on plants. For example, some might die overnight if subject to even 1 day of extreme heat above 100F, and leaf temperatures over 120F immediately scorches and kills plant cells. In most parts of the country, unless your greenhouse is at an east exposure (getting only morning sun), you are going to have to provide some shading for the structure.

Old-fashioned paste or whiting powder can be applied with a spray or paintbrush, but this is a bother and ugly looking. Instead, use moveable aluminum- or wood-slatted ventian blinds or bamboo rollups. They cost more than powders or paints, but they look better, are easy to install, and can be opened during periods of only bright light.

Plastic shading, like paint or powder, is also a bother and looks terrible. Use some nice curtains that break the sunlight yet allow some light through. Even better is special window trellage, which adds great charm to a building. (This is my preference, after trying other methods of shading.) Trellises can be built cheaply and installed with little effort; they will provide almost perfect light for plants as alternating shade and light is created.

Heating

Heating the greenhouse depends mainly where you live, the size of the greenhouse, and the design. Once greenhouse heating was a maze of pipes and problems, and only hot water heat was considered for plants. Today we know that many other types of heating are suitable. Installation and operation of the heating unit is not too difficult, but determining what kind of heating fuel to use—gas, oil, or electricity—can be tricky.

Before you select the heating system for your greenhouse, check local gas and electric rates. Decide which will be the most economical and then investigate specific systems. For my small greenhouse I used forced hot air heat by extending one duct from the house furnace. A professional installed the duct for $60. A small furnace with about three ducts (for the average greenhouse) would cost no more than $400.

The warm-air-gas-fired heater is popular for greenhouses; it has a safety pilot and thermostatic controls. You may have to provide masonry or metal chimneys so fumes are released outside. A nonvented heater does not need an outlet chimney; the combustible chamber is sealed and outside the greenhouse. The heater extends about 10 inches inside the greenhouse and needs only a 17- by 20-inch wall opening. Both types of heaters are approved by the American Gas Association (AGA) and are available through greenhouse dealers.

The warm-air-oil-fired heater is small, able to fit under a greenhouse bench. It will furnish sufficient heat for most average-sized greenhouses. It has a gun-type burner, a blower, a two-stage fuel pump, and full controls. This heater requires a masonry chimney or a metal smokestack above the roof.

Electric heaters are also satisfactory for small greenhouses. These units are automatic, built with a circulating fan, but heavy-duty electrical lines are necessary. The heater and thermostats should be installed by a professional in accordance with local electric codes.

See list of suppliers at the end of the book for greenhouse heaters.

SAVING HEAT

There are several ways to "store" heat in the greenhouses so you will not have to use so much fuel. These methods are relatively simple and involve using the right materials. For example, a concrete floor is a remarkable heat storer: it absorbs enough heat during the day (if the structure faces south) to keep the room warm a good part of the night, even in very cold climates. Masonry walls opposite the glass wall will also absorb the sun's heat and store it for night time radiation; even a wooden wall painted a dark color will help greatly to save on heating.

If you can afford it, use some thermopane, the insulating glass, in some areas of the greenhouse (perhaps on the north wall, where winds are generally strongest). Thermopane can save as much as 30 percent heat in the area, and even though its initial installation is more expensive than standard glass, in the long run it certainly pays for itself (see section on glass).

Once the greenhouse is built, landscape with hedges and shrubs at the sides where storms hit the hardest. This simple landscaping can effectively cut your

heating bills a great deal, and planting some low-growing trees or shrubs in double rows at the corner of the greenhouse will add to the beauty of the total area. The natural barriers will also screen out dust, pollution, and noise.

Another effective way of cutting down on heat bills is to install heavy drapery; this thwarts cold drafts and keeps the greenhouse quite warm at night without extensively turning up the thermostat. Or better yet, use inexpensive wooden shutters or rollup blinds. These help keep out cold, thus cutting down on artificial heating.

Weatherstripping, sold in packages at hardware stores, can and should be used to further keep cold air out and warm air in the greenhouse. These effective products are especially easy to apply to wooden windows. They can cut heat loss by about 10 percent, so do not discount them as a gimmick. In Chicago, I always used them on greenhouse windows and cut my fuel bill quite a bit. (Also see chapt. 7).

Insect Control

Even in the best managed greenhouse, some plants may be attacked by insects but there is no cause for alarm. If you catch insects before they have a foothold they are easy to eliminate. Thus, the main thing is to observe plants as you walk through the greenhouse; look for signs of insects. Most common plant insects are recognizeable on sight such as aphids, mealy bugs, spider mites, scale, slugs, and snails. If you cannot identify the insect, pick it off the plant, kill it, and mail it in a plastic Baggie to your local County Agricultural Agency or Extension Service (listed in phone book), so they can identify it for you and tell you how to cope with it.

Aphids are pear-shaped small soft-bodied insects with a tiny beak that pierces plant leaves and extracts sap. Aphids may be black, red, brown, or gray in color. Plants attacked by these insects lose vigor, may become stunted and leaves may curl or pucker.

Mealy bugs have soft segmented bodies dressed in cotton wax. They often appear in leaf axils and take sap from plants and especially are fond of young growth.

Spider mites are difficult to see but they do spin webs which often gives them away. Foliage attacked by spider mites turns pale and may become stippled around the injured parts.

Scale are tiny and oval and have an armored shell or scales covering their body. They stay in one spot and extract sap from the plant. Leaf as well as stem damage may result when plants have scale.

Thrips are chewers and are very small slender insects with two pairs of long narrow wings. Thrips are usually indicated by silver sheen on the leaves.

Slugs and snails are easily recognizeable and no description is necessary; they are most apt to be found under pots and in dark corners of the greenhouse.

There are many preventatives for pests named above and these come in the forms of dusts, powders or sprays. Systemics—insecticides applied to soil—are also offered, and protect plants from some chewing and sucking insects for 6 to 8 weeks. Malathion will help control most of the insects mentioned above; for slugs and snails use a snail bait without methaldehyde which is highly poisonous. Snare-All is relatively safe if used as directed. With all chemicals, keep them out of reach of children and pets (on a high shelf is good), and always follow directions on the package to the letter.

If you object to using poisonous chemicals near and around the house (and I do) you can try some old-fashioned remedies. These ways are not as thorough as chemicals and take repeated applications but they are safe and avoid noxious odors.

1. *Handpicking.* Hardly pleasant but it can be done with a toothpick.

2. *Soap and water.* For many insects such as aphids and mealybugs, a solution of 1/2 pound of laundry soap (not detergent) and water works fine.

3. *Alcohol.* Alcohol on cotton swabs will effectively remove mealybugs and aphids from plants. Apply directly to insects.

4. *Tobacco.* Use a solution of old tobacco from cigarettes seeped in water for several days. Apply with cotton swab; gets rid of scale.

5. *Water spray.* May sound in-

The heater for this greenhouse is at far right deftly camouflaged with a vine on lattice work. *(Photo by Clark Photo Graphics).*

effective, but works if used frequently and with strong enough force to wash away insects and their eggs.

6. *Wipe leaves frequently.* This simple step goes a long way to reduce insect problems in a greenhouse. It washes away eggs before they have a chance to hatch.

Maintenance

Any structure, including a greenhouse, needs periodic maintenance. If you check the greenhouse twice a year, you can remedy most problems with little effort or time. For example, foundations may develop cracks, but when caught in time they can be fixed by filling them in with appropriate compounds. If you are using glass for a covering, periodically check for broken panels and the glazing compound that holds the glass in place. If it is missing in a few places, replace it with more compound. In some cases complete reglazing with a new glazing compound may be best; if you have used putty instead of the newer glazing compounds, chances are it has become brittle with time and can be chipped away easily.

Repaint wooden members whenever it is needed. Do not neglect this because once excess moisture starts in wood it can cause havoc and travel quickly. If painting the inside of the greenhouse, clear out all plants rather than trying to do the job with plants intact; it is just too difficult, and paint fumes can harm plants.

Always check guttered and lipped grooves to be sure water is draining properly. Make any repairs immediately rather than waiting until a total replacement is necessary. Use a tar-based gutter paint for all gutters because it resists the extra moisture present in these areas.

7 Solar Greenhouses

A conventional greenhouse when properly located to receive the full effect of the sun is essentially a heat trap—a passive solar structure. Heat from the sun's rays is stored during the day and used by plants at night. This natural process can be helped somewhat by installing a concrete or heat-absorbing north wall opposite the south wall of glass. Or special back walls of rock or water-filled drums can be built; these walls act as a "radiator," releasing the trapped daytime heat. A more sophisticated solar greenhouse electrically pumps heated air into a storage area, but this active type of greenhouse is complex in design, is expensive to build, and has to be professionally planned and executed. In temperate climates, such as California, the passive types of greenhouses work fine, to trap heat. In cold-winter areas, however, such as Illinois, active solar greenhouses are the answer, with additional heating. (The basic construction of the foundation of a solar greenhouse is the same as for any greenhouse, as covered in earlier chapters.)

Insulation

No matter what kind of solar greenhouse you build, active or passive, the heat stored in it on sunny days will be lost unless the structure is as airtight as possible. Glass must be securely glazed, and weather stripping around windows and doors is essential to eliminate drafts (which also harm plants). But even in a tightly sealed greenhouse some heat is lost through the glazing material. An efficient and inexpensive way to keep heat is to staple 4-mil plastic, about 1 inch, under the glass; this reduces heat loss 30 to 40 percent because it creates an air space—the air-space principle is what double-glazed glass is all about. Thermopane is the ideal glazing material for greenhouses, but it is expensive.

Other insulation materials include rigid styrofoam panels and plastic bubble packs, but they are hard to install and so can be more trouble than they are worth.

The North Wall

The north wall is the important heat-retaining wall of your greenhouse—both heat and light will be wasted unless this wall is constructed of the proper material. The north wall should be covered with an insulating material that will absorb both heat and light. White rigid insulation panels fitted on the north wall will greatly reduce heat and light because white reflects rather than absorbs.

Fiberglass covered with plywood will properly absorb heat and light. Hollow concrete blocks as a north wall are excellent if you are just building a greenhouse; they retain an enormous amount of heat and thus act as an insulator. No additional heating apparatus is needed with hollow concrete blocks if you live in temperate climates.

Orientation

Whether an active or passive type, a solar greenhouse requires

COLD CLIMATE GREENHOUSE

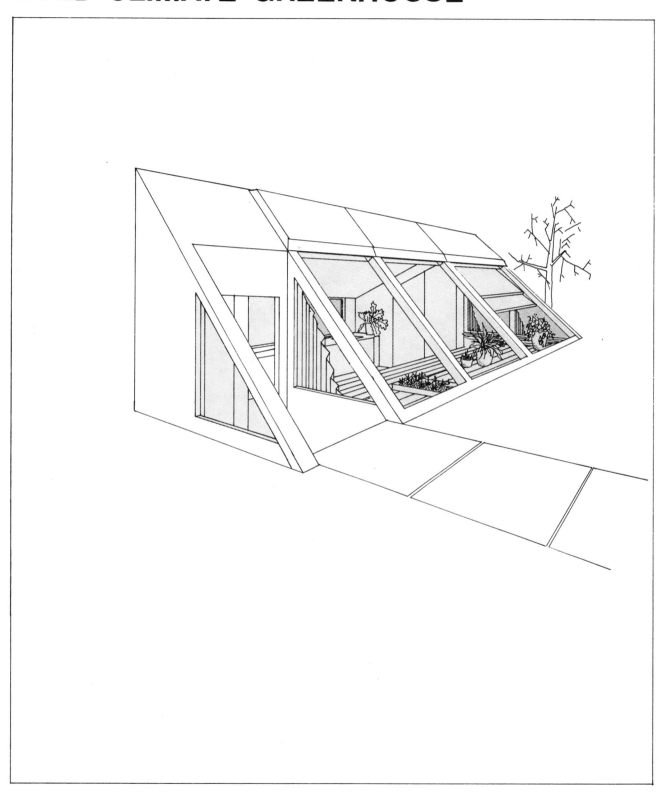

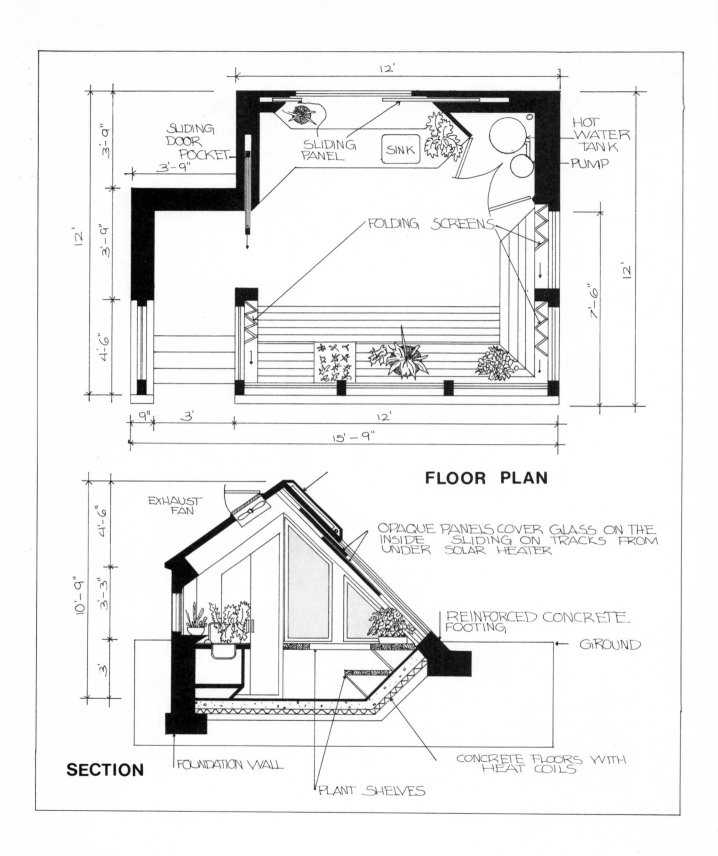

12'

3'-9"

SLIDING
DOOR
POCKET

3'-9"

12'

3'-9"

4'-6"

SLIDING
PANEL

SINK

FOLDING SCREENS

HOT
WATER
TANK

PUMP

12'

7'-6"

9"   3'

12'

15'-9"

FLOOR PLAN

EXHAUST
FAN

4'-6"

10'-9"

3'-3"

3'

OPAQUE PANELS COVER GLASS ON THE
INSIDE   SLIDING ON TRACKS FROM
UNDER SOLAR HEATER

REINFORCED CONCRETE
FOOTING

GROUND

SECTION

FOUNDATION WALL

PLANT SHELVES

CONCRETE FLOORS WITH
HEAT COILS

90

LEAN-TO GREENHOUSE

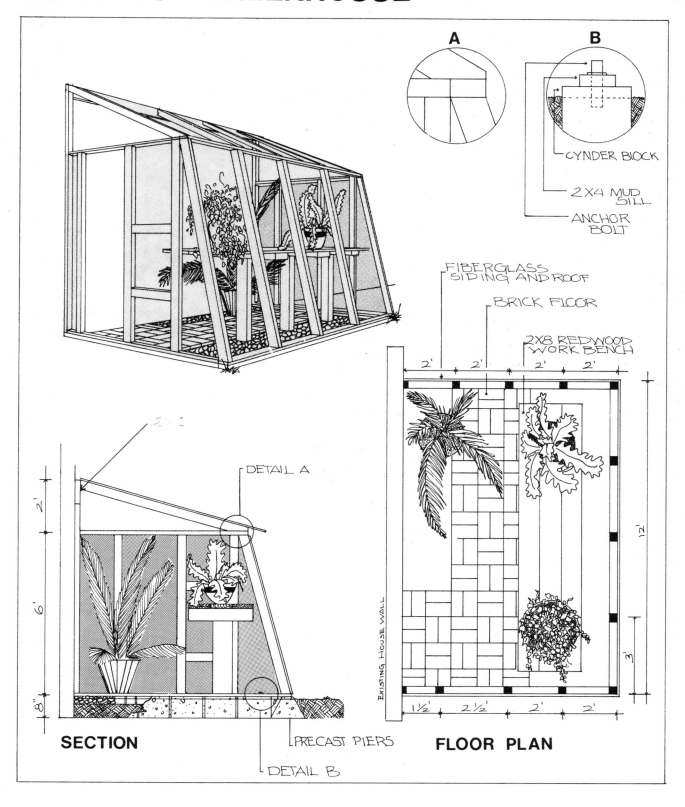

A

B

CYNDER BLOCK

2 X 4 MUD SILL

ANCHOR BOLT

FIBERGLASS SIDING AND ROOF

BRICK FLOOR

2X8 REDWOOD WORK BENCH

2' 2' 2' 2'

12'

3'

EXISTING HOUSE WALL

1½' 2½' 2' 2'

FLOOR PLAN

DETAIL A

2'

6'

8"

SECTION

PRECAST PIERS

DETAIL B

a southern exposure. If you try to determine the position of the greenhouse by simply looking at the sun, you could be way off because the sun moves around a great deal, depending upon the season. Find magnetic south by using a compass; a survey map will tell you how many degrees east or west from your site true south is. Add or subtract these degrees to find true south.

Be careful in planning the greenhouse location. Remember that in the winter the sun is low in the sky, whereas in the summer it is almost overhead. You want your greenhouse situated so that it receives the greatest possible amount and intensity of light during the winter, when daylight hours are few, and less light in summer, when overheating can be a problem. If you design your plant palace in accordance with the movement of the sun, you will get ultimate winter heating and summer cooling.

Any object that blocks sunlight from entering the greenhouse is an obstruction. Even an hour of sun lost in a day may necessitate turning on the artificial heat at night. It is fine to have a deciduous tree shading the greenhouse from late afternoon summer sun—this can be an asset. But a wall of evergreens 10 feet away could create a serious drawback because the trees or shrubs will prevent the sun from reaching the greenhouse. For best midwinter operation no more than 1 hour of sun can be lost to obstructions.

Greenhouse Size

It pays to be sensible about the size of the greenhouse. A general guideline that has proved successful in planning solar greenhouses is to allow the length to be about 1 1/2 to 2 times the width. A 10 x 16-foot lean-to allows sufficient growing room. If the width becomes greater than 10 feet, the roof is shallow, and heavier support beams must be used.

Plan your design to allow winter sunlight to strike well up on the back (north) wall of the greenhouse—7 feet is good. This will provide about one-third partial shading in the summer. The angle of the south wall should be close to perpendicular with the average solar noon angle of the sun in the coldest months. In the northern hemisphere this is from December to mid February.

At solar noon the optimum tilt for winter sun collection is about 50 degrees in the south and about 70 degrees in the north. A good formula for establishing the tilt of the south wall is the latitude + 35 degrees. The south face of the greenhouse should not be steeply tilted to the summer sun; if it is, you will have intense summer radiation, resulting in overheating.

Solar Additions

Many manufacturers are offering solar panels for installation in

This small greenhouse in a back yard is almost self sufficient; it is solar heated using a thermal storage area of water tanks. It is orientated south to the sun. *(Photo by Dean Luckhart).*

Another view of the small solar greenhouse. *(Photo by Dean Luckhart).*

Interior view of the solar greenhouse showing storage vats of water—water inside vats is heated by sun during day—heat is then used at night. *(Photo by Dean Luckhart).*

Attractive and in keeping with the house, this redwood and glass greenhouse faces south to utilize the sun to the maximum—as such it is a passive solar greenhouse.

greenhouses, homes, swimming pools and so forth. Because there are so many types of solar concepts I cannot recommend any single unit. Rather I urge you to study materials and brochures carefully and to ask neighbors who have had actual solar additions installed on their premises. And even when using solar energy remember that when the sun does not shine the system does not work; thus some type of additional heating is required.

An early version of a solar collector is the mattress type—really a sandwich of flattened polyvinyl chloride tubing with turbulators that tumble the water around. Newer units are copper or anodized aluminum panels. The most popular collector consists of copper tubes laid

on aluminum fins and covered with glass or a rigid plastic to insulate the tubing. Polyethylene tubing is also used in panels because it can take in heat from any angle. The glass collector is most efficient because it takes in radiant heat easily and does not lose it.

There are two types of solar energy: active and passive. The passive system consists of a thermal mass area where heat is stored during the day and then radiates back at night into the structure. An area of rocks or water filled drums is the thermal storage area. Active systems require pumps and panels (collectors) and are complex as well as costly, but also more efficient.

The passive solar system works well in most greenhouses

—it is a process of trapping and storing the sun's energy and it does cut down on heating costs. The most widely used thermal storage mass or "heat sink" is a 55-gallon drum painted a dark color to absorb heat. Do not let the barrels come in contact with glazing or exterior walls. Heat moves to cold and if barrels touch something the outside cold quickly drains heat from the barrels.

If you use rocks make wire cages to hold them—chicken wire works fine. Place the rocks like the barrels where they get maximum sunlight.

Panels come in various sizes and consult your local phone book for manufacturers and distributors. You will find them listed under the Solar headings.

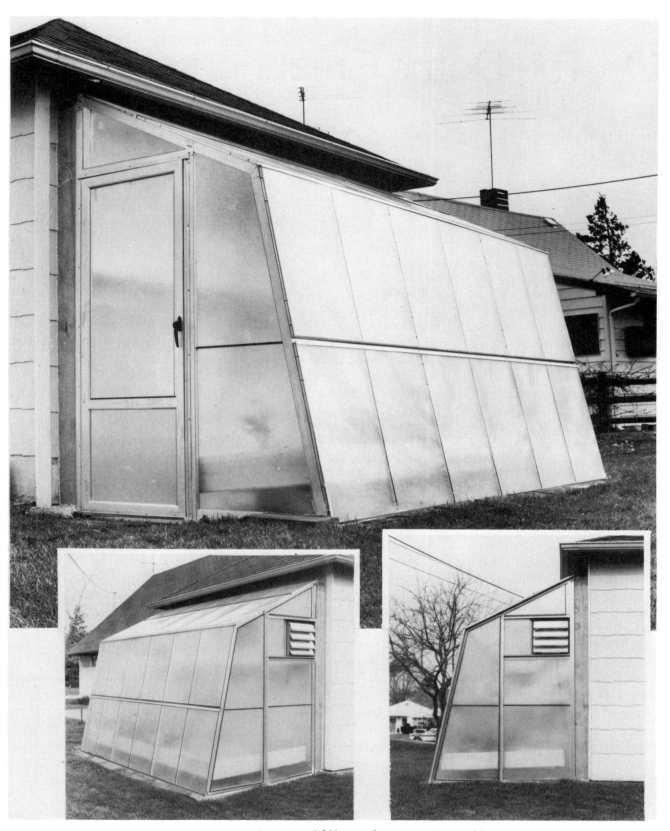

A commercial kit greenhouse manufactured by Vegetable Factory offers passive solar advantages; the unit is tightly sealed and saves heat.

8 The Dome Greenhouse

Geodesic domes used as greenhouses have become popular in the past few years because these structures are inexpensive to build, provide plants with maximum light, and offer ample growing height for plants. True, suitable benches and shelving have to be built, which is a project for only ambitious people, but once all the construction is done, the greenhouse will be a unique structure, well worth the time and effort and, if done properly, cheaper than a more conventional-type greenhouse. The domes can be complicated or easy to build, depending upon the design you choose: hexagon, octagon, polyhedron, and so forth. However, note that most dome greenhouses look awkward and out of place when placed right next to your house. But when connected to the house by a glass gallery, the greenhouse becomes a very desirable addition.

No matter which shape of dome you build, avoid making this greenhouse completely glass or completely flexible plastic because it will be too drafty and too difficult to glaze properly. Also, in an all-glass or all-plastic

dome greenhouse, too much light will be admitted and plants will burn. And heating in winter will be difficult, and in summer the dome will be hard to cool. Make the house small, and use thermopane or 1/4-inch plexiglass in one area and insulating board or a similar material in other areas, to conserve heat. The dome, like the lean-to, may have its foundation below ground or above ground with partial concrete foundation walls. Floors can be concrete or, to save money, cinders on earth.

Domes in year-round temperate climates can be built with a minimal support of posts or piers, but ideally the dome greenhouse should have a solid concrete foundation and preferably one solid concrete wall facing north (to retain heat). For ventilation, which is a must, the greenhouse should have several windows that can be opened. To further ensure against heat loss in winter, partially sink the dome, following the plan of an underground (pit) greenhouse as we describe in chapter 10.

The structural components (skeleton) of the dome can vary

from aluminum to various metal channels, but for the greenhouse a redwood skeleton is the best. The use of redwood, along with the recommended plexiglass, increases the cost of the dome greenhouse, but the combination of these materials produces a better, longer lasting structure than a conventional dome of all glass or all plastic.

Dome greenhouses are available in kits from some suppliers and the basic greenhouse design while of dome concept may be hexagonal or octagonal in shape. Unless you are very handy with tools and have a knowledge of carpentry it is best to use a kit rather than trying building a unit yourself. Kit prices for domes vary from $500 to $5000.

Foundations

The dome greenhouse, whether it is attached to the house by a glass gallery or left free-standing, should rest on a foundation, which can be poured concrete, concrete block, or brick. The footings of the foundation must extend from the

DOME GREENHOUSE

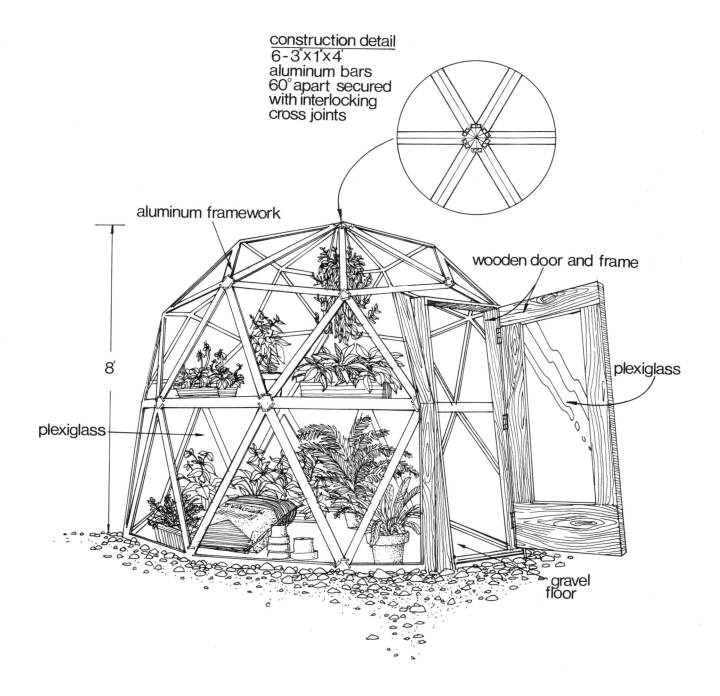

construction detail
6-3"x1"x4'
aluminum bars
60° apart secured
with interlocking
cross joints

aluminum framework

wooden door and frame

plexiglass

8'

plexiglass

gravel
floor

Interior shot of dome greenhouse; plants can be suspended from top moullions. Benches are used for interior for plants. *(Photo courtesy Redwood Domes).*

Kit greenhouses in dome design are now available and this structure shows the interlocking stut construction. *(Photo courtesy Redwood Domes).*

ground level to a few inches above the grade, down to or a few inches below the frost line. Frost lines for footings must be observed because alternating freezing and thawing of the ground will cause walls to crack, which is why building codes require that frost lines be observed. Call your local building department to find out the frost line in your area. As mentioned, greenhouse prices do not include foundation or footings.

You can hire a contractor to do most of the greenhouse construction, including digging out for the foundation and pouring the footings; you can install the foundation wall yourself. To do so, use premixed mortar, preparing only a little at a time. Do not use mortar when the tempera-

ture is below 40F because it will cause cracking in the wall. Add water to the mix, and with a hoe work the water throughout the mortar to get a heavy, pastelike consistency. If you are putting in a brick foundation wall, lay the bricks in a moist, never dry, mortar. Put the mortar on the footings for the first row of bricks. Use a trowel upside down to press ripples into the mortar; the ripples provide a good gripping surface for the bricks. Remove the excess mortar with the trowel. Lay brick one for the second row, and use the trimmed excess mortar to smear the edge of the next brick. Be sure to keep the rows of brick even and level. Remove all loose bits of mortar from the wall before the bricks have a chance to set. Cover the

wall with wet burlap for a few days to permit a slow cure and to prevent cracks. A few weeks later, clean the walls with muriatic acid and then hose down the walls thoroughly. In mild climates dome greenhouses can be installed on poured concrete slabs.

Floors

Although a dirt floor covered with gravel or crushed stones is adequate, a brick or tile floor is more attractive. Or use stepping stones (patio blocks) embedded in gravel; these materials retain moisture, and evaporation of water on the floor creates humidity in the greenhouse.

9 Artificial Light And Hydroponic Gardening

Even with a greenhouse and adequate light there are many gardeners who use artificial light to help plants grow. If you are in a region where sun is minimal, using supplemental flourescent light can greatly enhance plant growth. The same kind of setups used in indoor home growing are basically employed on the greenhouse as well: shelves and fixtures for lamps.

Another aspect of gardening that has received much interest in the last decade is growing plants without soil, in inert mixes, and supplying nutrients on a set schedule. This *hydroponic gardening* is fine for the person who has the time; if you have some space in the greenhouse, you might want to try your hand at hydroponics, especially for growing vegetables or cut flowers.

Fluorescent Lamps

Research has proved that a combination of fluorescent and incandescent light is beneficial to plant growth. (More about this in the later section How Plants Use Light.) Some gardeners do not use the incandescent lamps; they rely on fluorescents or use lamps specifically designed for plant growth. Fluorescent lamps come in an array of shapes, sizes, voltages, wattages, and temperature characteristics. And manufacturers give their lamps various trade names: cool white, daylight, warm white, natural light, soft white, and so on. However, these names can be misleading because a natural white lamp does not duplicate the sun's light, a daylight lamp does not actually duplicate daylight, and there is no difference to the touch between a cool white and a warm white lamp.

Cool white lamps are closest in providing the kind of light— red and blue—necessary for plant growth. Daylight lamps are high in blue but low in red, and warm white and natural white, although high in red, are deficient in blue. Fluorescent lamps come in 20, 40, and 72 watts, in standard lengths of 24, 48, 72, and 96 inches.

In addition to these standard fluorescent lamps, several companies have lamps designed solely for aiding plant growth. Among these lamps are Gro-Lux by Sylvania Lighting Company, Plant-Gro by Westinghouse Electric Company, and Vitima by Durolite Electric Company. With these lamps supplemental incandescent light is probably not needed because plant-growth lamps have both red and blue quotients of light.

There are also newer fluorescent lamps with high output. These lamps are grooved (Power Groove from General Electric Company), twisted in shape (Powertwist from Durolite Electric Company), or show no difference in shape and be designated as high output (HO) or very high output (VHO).

If you are making your own light setup, you will need reflectors to direct the light on the plants. You can buy metal reflectors, or paint the upper inside surface (where lamps are mounted) white. Incandescent lamps are available in a variety of wattages, but in combination with fluorescents it is best to use 15-or 20-watt lamps.

The cost of operating fluorescent and incandescent lamps for plants varies, depending on the rate charged by your local power company. The average cost per kilowatthour is less than 6 cents. Thus, a 100-watt (1 kilowatt) setup operating for 14 hours daily (the average time period for most plants) equals 14 kilowatthours— 84 cents a day, which is a bargain.

How Plants Use Light

Like a rainbow, the visible spectrum ranges from red to violet. Plants require blue, red, and far red to produce normal growth. Blue enables plants to manufacture carbohydrates; red controls assimilation and also affects plants' response to the relative length of light and darkness; far red works in conjunction with red in several ways: it controls seed germination, stem length, and leaf size by nullifying or reversing the action of the red rays.

Plants grow best when they receive sufficient levels of blue and red light, which are in standard fluorescent lamps, and far red light, which is in incandescent bulbs. (Some studies claim that the rest of the spectrum is necessary for optimum growth, but experiments have yet to produce incontrovertible facts.

Duration and Intensity of Light

A dark period is a crucial time for plants, and this means absolute darkness. Some plants

Flourescent lamps are used for supplemental lighting in this redwood span-and-plastic greenhouse. Lamps are generally used for seedlings but can also be effective for mature plants as well. *(Photo by Dean Luckhart).*

require a short day and some plants need a long day, and some plants are flexible or neutral in their light/dark needs; however, no one has so far determined the exact pattern for every plant. Most houseplants—caladium, calathea, coleus, hoffmannia, hoya, ficus, dieffenbachia, to name a few— are in the neutral category and will flower and set seed without precise timing of the dark period. Commercial growers must know about light and bloom time for seasonal sales, but most amateur greenhouse gardeners do not have to concern themselves with these technicalities.

Here are three helpful hints:

Even incandescent lamps as in this city garden under glass can be used to help plants grow; they furnish necessary red rays for growth and on cloudy days supply necessary light for plants. *(Photo by Pat Matsumoto).*

(1) For germinating seeds and cuttings, use 10 lamp watts per square foot of growing area.

(2) For plants like philodendrons, African violets, and most foliage plants, use 15 watts per square foot, and (3) for high-energy species like orchids, roses, and other flowering plants, 20 lamp watts per square foot are beneficial.

If you use incandescent light to furnish the vital far red rays that are lacking in most conventional fluorescent lamps, try the 4:1 ratio. For example, if you have 200 watts of fluorescent light, add 50 watts of incandescent light (five 10-watt bulbs). Increasing the incandescent ratio will create heat that will harm plants. Note that these rules are not set. Do experiment; trial-and-error is part of the adventure of growing greenhouse plants under lights.

Light intensity (measured in foot candles) is important to commercial growers because exact conditions are necessary for maximum production. But in the greenhouse it is not generally necessary to bother with foot-candle units. If the light intensity proves too strong for some of your plants, simply move the plants away from the light. Set them at the end zones of the lamps, where the light is less intense, or raise the adjustable reflector canopy. On the other hand, if light is not strong enough for some plants, move the plants closer to the light.

There is no set rule for how far a plant should be from fluorescent light. Observe your plants because they tell you when they are getting too much light (leaves are pale green) or when they are not getting enough (leaves are limp).

Timers

An automatic timer switch should be part of the greenhouse light equipment. These timers are convenient in that you can set them for a number of specific hours and know that the lamps will turn off automatically. Normal light periods for foliage plants are 12 to 14 hours; for flowering plants use lights for 16 to 18 hours daily. Timers are also valuable if you are going to be away from your indoor gardens for a few days because they can contol the daily light period.

Hydroponic (Soil-less) Gardening

Hydroponic gardening is growing plants in water solutions rather than soil. (The word hydroponics is derived from the Greek *hudor*, meaning water, and *ponos*, meaning work.) This soil-less gardening has been used mainly by commercial vegetable and cut flower growers; only recently have home gardeners recognized the advantages of hydroponic gardening.

Growing plants in water solutions is an inexpensive way of having all kinds of plants year-round, whether vegetables, flowers, or houseplants. And as a hobby it yields much satisfaction from a small amount of expense and effort. Healthy, aqua-grown plants are more lively than plants that may die because their soil has been depleted of nutrients. In water gardens plants are usually set into containers that hold aggregates (gravel, sand); water and nutrients are applied to the aggregates regularly. Or plants can be suspended in grids or holders (to keep them upright) in tanks or metal drums of nutrient solution. The aggregate method is better for noncommercial greenhouse gardening because it involves less work and preparation and looks better aesthetically than the suspension method.

The rate of application of the nutrients depends upon the kinds of plants you are growing. You can make your own nutrient solutions from chemicals, or buy prepackaged solutions from suppliers. In either case, you mix a specific amount of nutrient salts with a specific amount of water to feed plants with the necessary nutrients they need to grow.

NUTRIENT SOLUTIONS AND HOW TO USE THEM

Plants need a balanced diet of nutrients to prosper; in soil they utilize the nutrients from the soil. But in soil-less gardening you must supply the balanced diet to sustain plant growth. The kind of feeding formula or mixture you use depends on the kinds of plants being grown, the size of the container, the related factors like light, humidity, and air circulation. There are dozens of different hydroponic feeding formulas; just which one you use and how you apply it will determine your success with soil-less gardening.

The nutrients you will be working with (unless you buy prepackaged hydroponic food) are nitrogen, potassium, phosphorus, calcium, sulfur, and magnesium. The trace elements are iron, copper, zinc, manganese, and boron. Each element plays a very important part in the development of a plant.

FORMULAS

Although many different formulas have been developed through the years by hydroponic researchers, they all have the same objective: to supply plants with the vital foods they need to grow. Generally the actual choice of fertilizer salts is not as important as the balanced concentration of the necessary elements. In commercial growing, precise and stringent rules regarding solutions and their application are a must to produce the most in the least amount of time—a heavy, good crop. However, in greenhouse culture a few mistakes will not cause

This homemade greenhouse is a handsome design and top light is limited to two skylights. In winter supplemental lighting is used to help plants grow. *(Photo by Jack Kramer).*

A handsome door is the entrance to an hydroponic greenhouse. *(Photo by Dean Luckhart).*

undue harm. Your plants will soon let you know if your chemical formulas are awry; the symptoms of over- or under-feeding (unbalanced proportions of nutrients salts) are discussed later. Just as soil mixes vary in nutrient content, so do water solution formulas. You will have to experiment to achieve the final formulas that work for your plants in your greenhouse conditions.

Whether you buy your nutrient mixes readymade or blend your own at home depends on your personal choice. Being naturally curious, I prefer to weigh out my own nutrient salts on a kitchen scale, mix them together and store them, and use them as I need them for the plants. It is also cheaper than buying commercial hydroponic foods.

For general use the following mixtures will provide excellent results for most plants:

Packaged Chemicals or Salts*	Nutrients Supplied	Amount of Each (Ounces)
Sodium nitrate	Nitrogen	10
Potassium sulfate	Potassium, sulfur	3½
Superphosphate	Phosphorus, calcium	5
Magnesium sulfate (Epsom salts)	Magnesium, sulfur	3
Iron sulfate	Iron	¼

*Use approximately 5 teaspoons of formula to 5 gallons of water.

Another mixture, recommended by the United States Department of Agriculture, is:

Packaged Chemicals or Salts*	Nutrients Supplied	Amount of Each (Ounces)
†Ammonium sulfate	Nitrogen, sulfur	1½
Potassium nitrate	Nitrogen, potassium	9
Monocalcium phosphate	Phosphorus, calcium	4
Magnesium sulfate (Epsom salts)	Magnesium, sulfur	6
Calcium sulfate	Calcium, sulfur	7
Iron sulfate	Iron	Pinch

*Use approximately 5 teaspoons of formula to 5 gallons of water.
†Or sodium nitrate

This dome type greenhouse is for hydroponic growing; plants are grown in plastic trays in gravel on raised platforms. Tomato plants can be seen at left.

In the above mixtures, the trace or minor elements such as manganese, boron, zinc, copper, and minute amounts of other elements will probably be supplied by the impurities in the water supply. However, the commercial or packaged chemicals will already contains these minor elements. Thus it is unnecessary to add them to the solution. However, if you use pure-grade chemicals in making solutions, you will have to add some manganese sulfate, copper sulfate, boric acid crystals, and iron chelate (1 teaspoon). Add 1/3 fluid ounce to 10 gallons of water. Boric acid crystals dissolve in boiling water; manganese and copper dissolve in hot water.

Here is a breakdown of the main packaged chemicals or salts and what they supply to plants. Sodium nitrate is the usual source of nitrogen in nutrient solutions and has approximately 15 percent nitrogen. The sodium is not required by plants but appears to have no bad effects on plants. Potassium nitrate supplies both potassium and nitrogen but may be expensive. It contains about 13 percent nitrogen and 44 percent potash.

Potassium sulfate gives potassium to plants and contains about 50 percent. Superphosphate is the principal source of phosphorus; it contains 16 to 18 percent phosphorus. Magnesium sulfate (Epsom salts) is the cheapest form of magnesium (16 percent).

The following trace elements, when not supplied as impurities in the water or chemicals, are usually added as sulfates: copper sulfate, manganese sulfate, zinc sulfate, and boron (derived from boric acid crystals).

PREPARING AND APPLYING SOLUTIONS

To prepare the solution, weigh out amounts on a kitchen scale, and then put them one by one into a bowl or other container. Mix the ingredients together well, using a wooden spoon or a pestle—the idea is to break down any lumps. The mixture is completed when you have a fine powder. Now store the mixture in a dry container and cover the container; never let the nutrients get damp or wet before storing. Also, all individual fertilizers, tools, and containers should be absolutely dry. If you want to make a larger amount of nutrients, simply multiply all ingredients by 2, 3, and so on.

Add small amount of the formula to water, generally 5 teaspoonfuls of formula to 5 gallons of water for the completed nutrient solution. (If you would rather not prepare your own solutions, buy the commercially packaged hydroponic mixtures from chemical house, nurseries, and so forth. Follow the directions on the package to the letter. Do not try to substitute packaged fertilizes such as 10-10-5 for solutions because they do not contain all necessary ingredients for good hydroponic growing.

Once the container is set up and plants are in place, apply the first application of nutrient fertilizer to the surface of the aggregate. To avoid disturbing the aggregate, use the old-fashioned type of watering can, one with a metal spout that has many small holes in the spout. Sprinkle evenly and thoroughly so the solution penetrates all parts of the aggregate. (The aggregate should be like a moist sponge.) The rate of application of the solution depends on climatic conditions and the plants being grown. Vegetables and flowers require more frequent applications than, say, houseplants. In very hot, dry areas, more solution is necessary than in damp, cool places. Generally, for most plants use two or three applications a week. In spring and summer, plants may need new solution every other day. In the fall, once or twice a week is sufficient, and in the winter, once a week is enough.

Make sure the growing medium never dries out. On the other hand, be careful that the medium never becomes waterlogged; that is, there should be no excess water standing above the aggregate surface line. Every third day or so (depending on the size of the container), remove the drainage plugs and let all unused water solution inside the bottom of the container seep out into a saucer or tray. Discard the unused water to remove spent nutrients and toxic salts and to move air through the aggregate from the open holes to the surface of the medium, which benefits roots.

If you are using too much water and solution, your plants will soon tell you: they will start wilting because they are waterlogged. If this occurs, once every 2 weeks remove the plugs and leach the aggregate gently by pouring clear water onto the surface. Repeat several times to really remove all toxic salts. (See also the nutrients deficiency symptoms at the end of this chapter.)

pH

The pH indicates the amount of acid or alkalinity in the nutrient solution. Most plants prefer a neutral medium (pH 7); a pH below 7 indicates acidity, and a pH above 7 indicates alkalinity. In alkaline mediums, potash becomes less and less effective and eventually becomes locked in and of no used to the plant. In very acid mediums, the element aluminum becomes so active that it can become toxic to plants. Acidity controls three main functions: (1) it governs the availability of the food in the medium; (2) it determines which bacteria thrive in the medium; and (3) to some extent it affects the rate at which roots can take up moisture and leaves can manufacture food.

Raising or lowering the pH of soil can be a difficult process and generally must be done over a period of time. But in soil-less gardening it is far easier for you to adjust the pH to the optimum required for plants. To determine the pH of your growing medium—to be sure you are applying correct amounts of solution—use litmus paper (sold at suppliers). All you have to do is match the color of the test strip with an indicator chart.

Note: If the pH of the solution is maintained at approximately 5.5 to 6.0, a reasonable concentration of ammonia can be used without injury to plants. When the pH is increased, the rate of entry of ammonia into the plant is also increased, and the plant may become injured.

The best pH for most vegetable crops is between 6.6 and 6.8. If the pH is too low, add small amounts of phosphoric acid; if it is too high, add caustic potash. Add micronutrient solutions after new solutions have been pH-adjusted. This should adjust the pH of the growing medium in about 1 week.

NUTRIENT DEFICIENCY SYMPTOMS

Because plants live or die depending on the nutrient solution, you must know these eight general plant deficiency symptoms so you can make necessary adjustments in your formula:

1. If plants have light green foliage and growth seems stunted, or if leaves become almost yellow, you must add more nitrogen.
2. If there is delayed growth and the lower foliage turns yellow or very dark in color, the plants are not getting enough phosphorus.
3. If lower leaves are mottled near tips and margins and become brown, plants need more potassium.
4. If leaves curl or pucker, plants are not getting enough magnesium.
5. If plants have poor bloom and spots appear on leaf surfaces, plants are not getting enough manganese.
6. If leaves are very light green and plants are somewhat limp, the plants need more sulfur.
7. If leaves, especially young ones, are brown at tip or margins, plants need more calcium.
8. If stems are brittle or young leaves are stunted, plants need more boron.

AERATION

Aeration of the growing medium is vital if you want healthy plants. Oxygen must be present in the medium so a vigorous and healthy root system can grow. A poorly aerated medium retards root formation, and the plant becomes chlorotic through lack of iron because this element appears to be absorbed only by new roots. If the plant cannot absorb nutrients because of poor aeration, starvation symptoms occur: lack of color in leaves, to the point that they become dull and gray looking. Also, the plant wilts in bright light as transpiration becomes more rapid than absorption of water by the poorly developed roots.

Aeration also effects to some degree the amount of potassium absorbed by the plant. In a compacted medium carbon dioxide accumulates and harms plants.

10 Underground Greenhouses

The underground, or pit greenhouse, has been around for decades and is a viable self-heating type of place to grow plants. It is an even-span glass structure with an insulated roof. The pit greenhouse can be constructed against a house wall (attached lean-to) or be a detached A frame; the roof should always be at a 45 degree angle and facing south. This greenhouse is 4 or 5 feet deep and lined with concrete block or concrete. The floor is dirt, to absorb warmth from the sun. The steep pitch of the roof allows a maximum amount of interior air to be heated by the sun so that enough heat is locked in during the night, thus maintaining favorable temperatures—rarely below freezing—for plants.

Of course, the structure will vary somewhat depending on where you live. For example, in the mild climates of Mississippi or Georgia the need for over-the-glass insulation is minimal, but in Chicago or New York, where there is frequent subzero winter weather, insulation in the form of straw or wooden blinds over the glass on very cold nights is necessary.

Preparing to Build the Pit Greenhouse

When you plan the construction of your pit greenhouse, you must take into account certain practical considerations before lifting even one shovelful of dirt. Space is the prime factor, followed in quick order by location of the greenhouse and the installation of proper drainage facilities. Last, though perhaps first to some people, is cost. A small pit greenhouse rarely costs more than $400, which is an insignificant expense when you consider the amount of growing you can do.

None of these practical considerations are really formidable, but there is one part of the construction you should be warned about now: digging the excavation. This does not cost must money, but it takes quite a bit of muscle. If you can hire out this work, do so. I started my own excavation, but when it got 2 feet down it proved too much for me, so I had to bring in additional hands.

Space and Location

With land at a premium today, you must carefully plan your available growing space. Here is where pit gardening is ideal, because even in a small area you can have a garden below ground level. A lean-to structure connected to a house wall is a space-saving form of pit garden, taking about only 8 feet along the side of the house. Such space, generally unused, often exists between adjacent houses, so even if you have hardly any land there is little excuse for not having a pit garden.

You can also convert a small part of your cellar to a pit greenhouse, with minimum expense and great productivity. Just built a suitable opening and encase it with glass sash or, even better, a plastic bubble (see list of suppliers, page 137) placed against the house wall.

My underground garden is only 8 X 12 feet, hardly a large area, yet I can grow an assortment of vegetables, mushrooms, flowers for cutting, bulbous plants, and seeds. I also use the garden as a

PIT GREENHOUSE

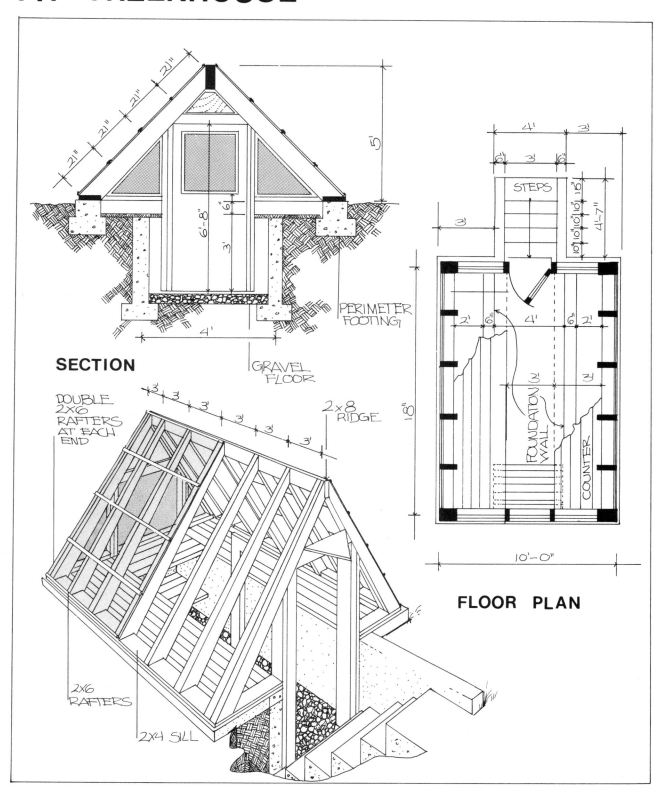

SECTION

PERIMETER FOOTING

GRAVEL FLOOR

DOUBLE 2X6 RAFTERS AT EACH END

2X8 RIDGE

2X6 RAFTERS

2X4 SILL

STEPS

FOUNDATION WALL

COUNTER

FLOOR PLAN

10'-0"

PREFABRICATED PIT GREENHOUSE

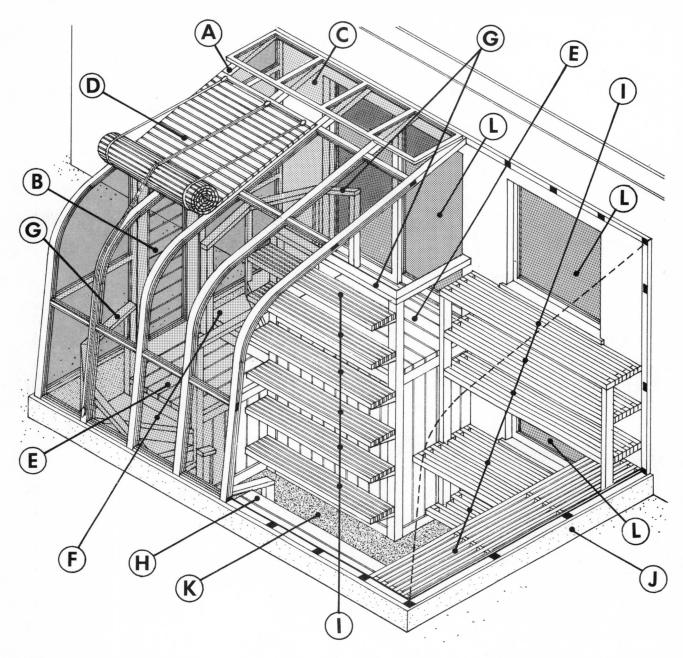

(A) aluminum and glass prefabricated greenhouse (B) door with jalousie window (C) vents
(D) aluminum roll-up shades (E) landings: 2×6 (F) steps (G) handrails: 2×4 and 4×4
(H) workbench: 2×6 (I) shelves: 2×2 (J) reinforced concrete foundation (K) gravel
floor (L) existing windows and sliding glass door

PREFABRICATED PIT GREENHOUSE

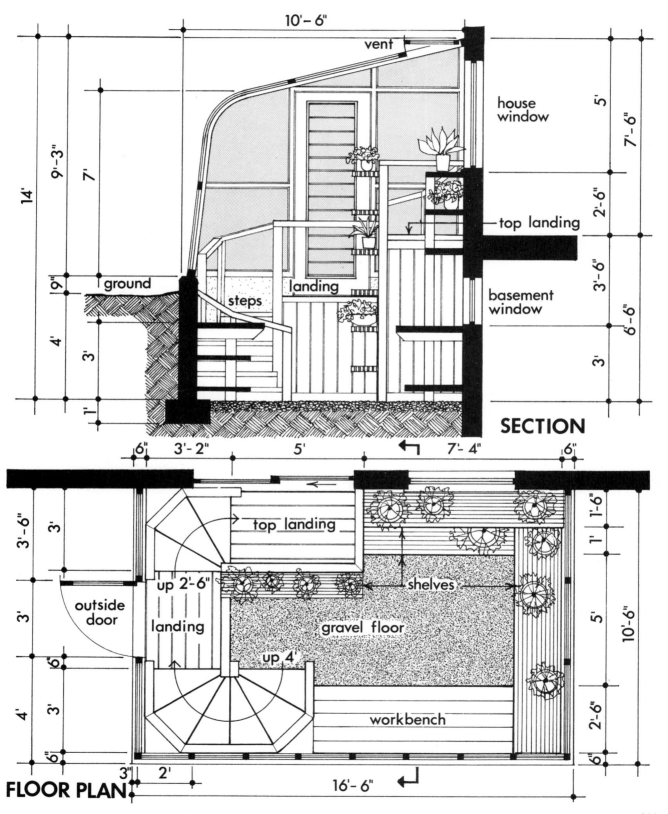

SECTION

FLOOR PLAN

storage place for bulbs during their rest period.

In an 8 X 12 garden you can have two rows of benches, one on each side, with several hanging plants, trellises for climbing plants like cucumbers and squash, and perhaps a few rambler roses for color along the end of one wall. Under the benches you can have shelves for growing shade-loving plants (begonias, for example) or for cultivating vegetables.

If you want to grow a few fruit trees in espalier style, that is, trained on a wall in the pit, make the greenhouse somewhat larger than 8 X 12 because fruit trees need some space even when espaliered. If you practice succession planting, you can have blooming plants all year long—not many, but certainly enough to decorate the home.

To use the sun's energy as a heat source, the greenhouse has to face south, as we mentioned, because there is no other way to get the necessary heat, unless you add artificial heat to the greenhouse. If you do use artificial heat, the greenhouse of course may face east or west. But no matter what exposure the pit greenhouse has, try to have a natural barrier of plants at the end that gets the severest winds. You can determine which end this is simply by observing from which direction the storms usually come. In my area storms come from the northwest, so on that side of the pit I have barriers of hedges and trees. This reduces the wind factor considerably and helps keep the heat in the greenhouse.

Basic construction details of an underground greenhouse on author's property. Concrete block is used for foundation; framing is basically 2 x 4's. *(Photo by Jack Kramer).*

Closeup shot of underground greenhouse. *(Photo by Jack Kramer).*

Excavation

In most cases the pit must be excavated to at least 4 feet, with a width and length of 8 feet each. If the pit is in flat ground, the soil has to be hauled away, usually by wheelbarrow, which is an arduous process. If you place the pit in the side of a hill or in uneven ground, you will have to do some grading. Use the excavated earth to grade the sides of the pit so you will not have to laboriously haul the soil away. Make the excavation large enough—at least 8 feet across— to allow for the construction of walls to hold the earth in place.

Pouring cement walls requires wooden forms and a great deal of work. I used the easier method of building with hollow concrete blocks, with mortar between them. Also, the hollow concrete block wall provides better insulation than a solid concrete wall. You can make walls of stone, but it really takes effort and skill to lay a perfect stone wall.

Digging the hole for the pit is the toughest part of construction, so try and get help; two or three people can dig the pit in 1 day. Remember to use the excavated soil to grade the sides of the pit.

Drainage

First study your property's topography to determine just where and how the pit should be constructed. Then plan suitable drainage facilities. You must install proper drainage facilities because water draining into the underground greenhouse can create serious problems. It is easy to install these facilities at the time of building, but impossible afterward. Run drain tiles along each side of the pit, or install them underground, so the water will leach out in a bottom area. Drain tile is just clay pipe, available in 3- to 5-inch diameters. Install the tiles in a trench 12 inches wide and 10 inches deep along each outside wall, and cover the trenches with gravel. These drainage lines should continue to lower ground.

Some people use only a layer of pebbles (about 4 or 5 inches) over the earth as a drain, but this works only in very level areas. If the terrain is hilly, you have to use drain tiles.

Usually the drainage ditches are enough precaution against flooding, but if you live where the water table is naturally high, you may need some mechanical help to keep the pit from turning into a wading pool. Use a small electric sump pump, or dig a well and fill it with stone to serve as a drain.

Ventilation

The pit greenhouse must have a ventilating fan(s) in the roof. You can buy a fan at a building-supply store. Fans come in several sizes, so make the opening fit one of these sizes. A small rotating electric fan run at low speed and set inside is also a good idea. You want to keep air circulating in the greenhouse—not a gale, just a gentle flow.

Interior of the underground greenhouse or sun pit; excavation is 48 inches below ground level. *(Photo by Jack Kramer).*

In Illinois, this partially sunken greenhouse works well even in severe winters. The underground construction saves on heat. *(Photo by Ray McCoullough).*

Partially sunk greenhouse inspring. *(Photo by Ray McCoullough).*

Winter Protection

For all-year use, to get the most out of the greenhouse you must give the pit greenhouse winter protection. The pit itself (the excavation) requires no insulation, but the structure above the ground does—the north eave if an A frame or where the greenhouse joins the house if a lean-to. Just what you do to insulate and how much insulation you use depends on the part of the country you live in. The idea is to keep the pit temperature from falling below freezing. Use double-glazed glass (now available at reasonable prices) for the eaves because it provides good insulation. The glassed area must be built carefully to prevent leaks and drafts. To further prevent heat loss, cover the inside surface of the glass with plastic, such as polyurethane, leaving a 2-inch air space between the plastic and the glass. This procedure will almost eliminate the need for other winter insulation, even in cold climates.

In relatively mild areas it is easy to provide any extra insulation: merely use shutter blinds during the evening. However, in very cold climates you have to use hay, straw, heavy tarps, boards, and so on to furnish additional protection. But even with these coverings some additional artificial heat may be necessary. If so, use a small plug-in electric heater, with the thermostat set at 40F. You can also use burlap or canvas bags loosely filled with leaves; to keep the leaves from settling to the bottom of the bags, sew quilting in place. Heavy boating canvas is also good additional winter protection.

If you can afford them, install wooden rollups over the glass. These heavy blinds, available from greenhouse suppliers, easily roll up and down. In winter, roll up the blinds at about 10 A.M.; lower them at dusk.

11 Planning the Window Greenhouse

When you add a window greenhouse to your home, you capture the outdoors indoors. You do not have to worry about whether there are trees and shrubs outside or gray concrete surrounding you. You can provide your own natural scene. And in this space you can grow plants all year because of the simulated conditions maintained there.

What you can grow depends on space; there is no other limitation. You can grow orchids, bromeliads, vegetables, herbs, even a few annuals and perennials. The kinds of plants feasible are not a problem—but space will be, so when planning the greenhouse take this factor into consideration; or install two window greenhouses.

You can build (or have built) your own window greenhouse, or buy a prefabricated one. Building a greenhouse is not difficult, as you will see from the several working drawings of different types of window greenhouses in this book. These greenhouses accommodate almost any type or size of window opening.

Practical Considerations

If you own your home, there is no problem as to whether the greenhouse may be attached to a window. However, in a rented apartment you should—and usually have to—secure permission from the owner; here a greenhouse that can be disassembled (and most window greenhouses can be) is the best answer. Usually a landlord will not object to the greenhouse because it adds to the property's appearance. And today even the most hardened superintendents have their own collections of greenery, so they are receptive to the idea of tenants having gardens.

If you build your own unit (or have it built), consider the materials available. Is metal better than wood, or is wood the answer? To many people wood is the ideal choice because it is natural looking and imparts a unified impression that never clashes with a building. On the other hand, metal has its pluses: it is rustproof and sleek in appearance. Note though that metal is harder to work with than wood.

You can buy metal channels at supply yards and wood molding at lumber dealers. The best wood for your greenhouse is redwood because it resists weathering; the best metal is aluminum because it resists rust. The wooden window greenhouse is about 25 percent less expensive to make than the metal unit. The average wooden greenhouse for a 24 X 30-inch opening should not cost more than $100, and will probably cost less. Metal units run about $125.

Should you buy a ready-made unit and assemble it, or make your own? If you do not have the time to make your own greenhouse or are not handy with tools, get a prefabricated unit. Prefab units come knocked down, with all pieces included, and you put them together by following the accompanying instruction sheets. If you buy a prefab greenhouse, ask if it can be installed from the inside, and always first determine whether

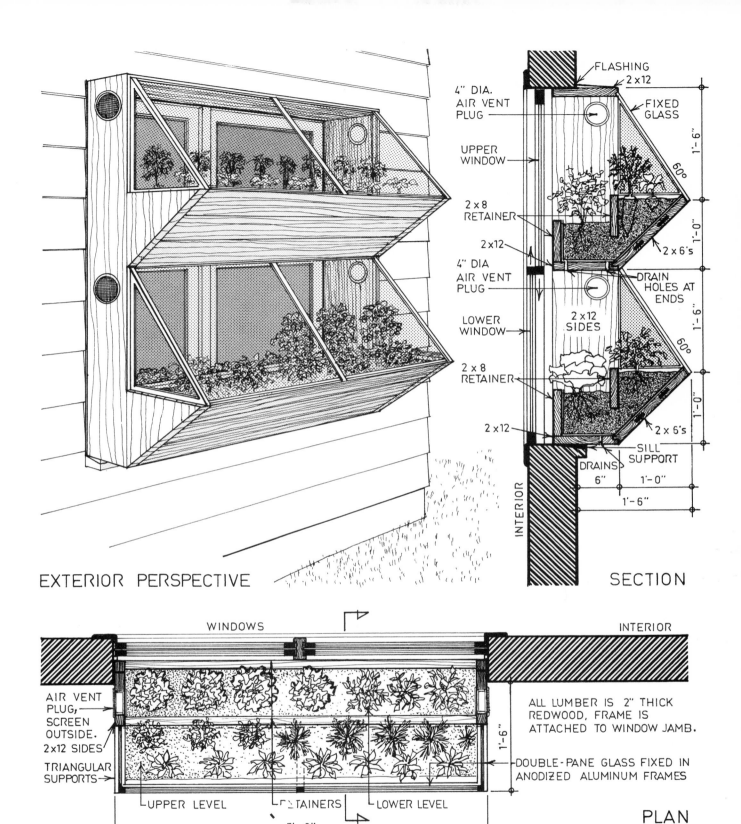

EXTERIOR PERSPECTIVE

FLASHING
2 x 12

4" DIA. AIR VENT PLUG

FIXED GLASS

UPPER WINDOW

2 x 8 RETAINER

2 x 12

4" DIA AIR VENT PLUG

2 x 6's

DRAIN HOLES AT ENDS

LOWER WINDOW

2 x 12 SIDES

2 x 8 RETAINER

2 x 12

2 x 6's

SILL SUPPORT

DRAINS

INTERIOR

1'-6"

1'-0"

1'-6"

1'-0"

60°

60°

6"   1'-0"

1'-6"

SECTION

WINDOWS

INTERIOR

AIR VENT PLUG, SCREEN OUTSIDE.

2 x 12 SIDES

TRIANGULAR SUPPORTS

UPPER LEVEL

RETAINERS

LOWER LEVEL

5'-0"

1'-6"

ALL LUMBER IS 2" THICK REDWOOD, FRAME IS ATTACHED TO WINDOW JAMB.

DOUBLE-PANE GLASS FIXED IN ANODIZED ALUMINUM FRAMES

PLAN

Saw-tooth Window Greenhouse

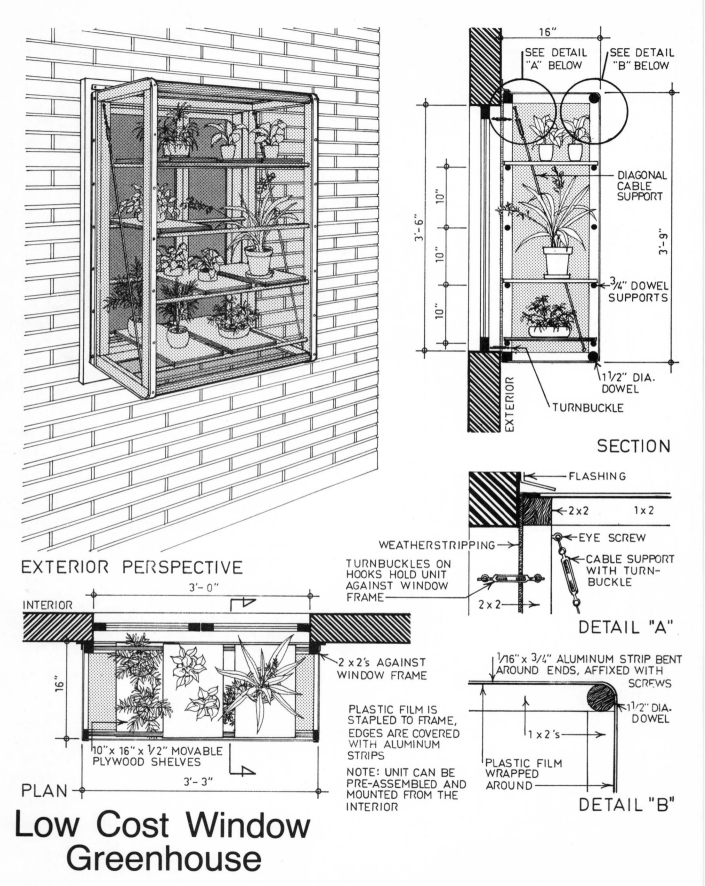

EXTERIOR PERSPECTIVE

16"

SEE DETAIL "A" BELOW

SEE DETAIL "B" BELOW

DIAGONAL CABLE SUPPORT

3'-6"

10"

10"

10"

3'-9"

3/4" DOWEL SUPPORTS

1½" DIA. DOWEL

TURNBUCKLE

EXTERIOR

SECTION

FLASHING

2 x 2   1 x 2

WEATHERSTRIPPING

TURNBUCKLES ON HOOKS HOLD UNIT AGAINST WINDOW FRAME

EYE SCREW

CABLE SUPPORT WITH TURN-BUCKLE

2 x 2

DETAIL "A"

INTERIOR

3'-0"

2 x 2's AGAINST WINDOW FRAME

16"

10" x 16" x ½" MOVABLE PLYWOOD SHELVES

3'-3"

PLAN

PLASTIC FILM IS STAPLED TO FRAME, EDGES ARE COVERED WITH ALUMINUM STRIPS

NOTE: UNIT CAN BE PRE-ASSEMBLED AND MOUNTED FROM THE INTERIOR

1/16" x 3/4" ALUMINUM STRIP BENT AROUND ENDS, AFFIXED WITH SCREWS

1½" DIA. DOWEL

1 x 2's

PLASTIC FILM WRAPPED AROUND

DETAIL "B"

Low Cost Window Greenhouse

you must remove the window frame or if you can leave it in place. With most prefab models the window frame can stay in place, but some units are so designed that it must be removed.

Perhaps the most logical place for the window greenhouse is the kitchen because people spend a good deal of time there and a lovely green scene boosts the spirits early in the morning. And of course watering plants in the kitchen is convenient. The disadvantage in placing the greenhouse in the kitchen is that most kitchens have only one window; fresh air will be blocked when the window greenhouse is in place. If this is not objectionable, then the kitchen is the first choice.

The second best location for a window greenhouse is the bathroom. Plants look good in bathrooms, softening the sometimes harsh lines or sterile colors, and water is only an arm's length away.

A living or dining room does not work well with a greenhouse unless the unit is custom designed to look like part of the building rather than a tacked-on afterthought. But if the greenhouse is designed to coordinate with the rest of the architecture, it can be very handsome. Just remember to create a marriage of indoors and outdoors by putting some potted plants on the floor or at the sides of the window to create balance and proportion.

Cellars or basements should not be ignored because these areas are fine places for greeneries. This was where my first window greenhouse ultimately took shape; it added a beauty to

The author's window greenhouse; it is 1/4 inch thick acrylic with glass shelves. Size is 48 inches across x 68 inches high. Bromeliads and other house plants grow lavishly inside. *(Photo by Jerry Bagger).*

the sterile basement and was a perfect retreat, a hidden place to work with plants.

The easiest installation of any window greenhouse is at ground level because, if necessary, you can work on the outside without ladders. If you live in a high-rise apartment building, the unit must be assembled from the inside, which is possible with most (but not all) greenhouse models.

Growing Conditions

Just what will the conditions be inside your window greenhouse? If the unit is built and installed properly, conditions will be similar to those in a regular greenhouse. That is, the temperature will be between 70° and 75 °F by day and 60 to 65° at night, and the humidity will be between 30 and 60 percent—ideal

Side view showing construction of window greenhouse and attachment to house with ledger strips. *(Photo by Jerry Bagger).*

conditions for hundreds of plants.

The greenhouse should be in a south, east, or west window, where there is ample light. But if other buildings interfere with the sunlight or the greenhouse must occupy a north window, there are numerous plants that can grow in shady places. With a reasonable amount of light, favorable temperatures, sufficient humidity, and correct watering, you will be able to have fresh and cheerful greenery and bloom all year long.

Constructing the Window Greenhouse

Almost anyone can nail and saw and insert glass or plastic. The main problem in window greenhouse construction is attaching the unit to the window; some expertise is needed here because you must have a perfect seal.

ATTACHING THE GREENHOUSE TO THE WINDOW

It is most important that the seal be free of leaks, cracks, or openings of any kind. You want the greenhouse to fit flush into the window, like a letter in an envelope. Sealing tapes and compounds are available if you should find after construction that there are some leaks.

LEDGER STRIPS

To attach the greenhouse properly you will need top, bottom, and side ledger strips. These strips are generally of 1 x 3-inch lumber; they form the greenhouse frame. The greenhouse

A homemade redwood and glass window greenhouse where all kinds of house plants thrive. Slatted shelves are efficient and allow air to enter pots. Ventilation is controlled by inner window which can be opened or closed. *(Photo by Matthew Barr).*

slots into the frame and is secured with screws or nails.

FLASHING

To secure a perfect seal between the house wall and greenhouse, some type of flashing—usually sheet metal or galvanized metal—should be used. Apply the material under the ledger strips.

BRACING

Bracing is not usually needed for small units, but for any unit over 24 x 36 inches screw or toenail in 2 x 4-inch braces at a 45-degree angle.

VENTILATION

If you do not make a hinged top for your greenhouse so you can regulate ventilation within, drill a 4-inch hole in each side of the greenhouse so air can circulate. Fit the holes with hardware cloth in summer; fill them with wooden stoppers in winter if necessary.

SNOW PROTECTION

In some climates the weight of snow might be damaging to the greenhouse roof. A pitched roof helps but still may not alleviate problems with very heavy snow, so if you live in a severe winter climate be sure this portion of the window greenhouse is well constructed so it can hold additional weight if necessary.

TOOLS

The basic hand tools needed for building your window greenhouse are the same ones you probably have on hand for home carpentry work: hammer, screwdrivers, drills, pliers, plane, saws. You do not need any other tools for your construction.

Materials

LUMBER

Use redwood or kiln-dried cedar heartwood for greenhouse frames because these are the only woods that resist moisture, decay, and insects. If you use woods like Douglas fir or pine, you must protect them from moisture with a sealing agent (sold at paint stores).

The amount of lumber required for your window greenhouse depends on the size of the structure, but basically you need a 2 X 4-inch corner posts, rabbeted to accept the appropriate thickness of glass or acrylic, and side and base rails. (What you are doing is building a frame for the glass or acrylic.) Or you can use prerabbeted picture molding, which has indentations to hold glass or acrylic.

For a glass greenhouse, make the basic frame and then install the glass. Slant the top of the greenhouse so rain will run off and the glass will catch as much sun as possible. Attach an exterior-grade plywood base. With an acrylic unit, first cement the sides and front; use ½-inch exterior-grade plywood for a base. Attach this rectangular box to the window, then add the top.

To attach either unit to the window, place 2 x 6-inch boards flat against the house wall on all four sides and bolt the boards in place. These are the anchor boards for the greenhouse frame. Small openings can be caulked with glazing compound.

ALUMINUM

Aluminum is used mainly for prefab window greenhouse frames because it is relatively inexpensive, lightweight, and sturdy. Also, it does not warp or rot and does not require a protective coat of paint. But aluminum has two major drawbacks: it looks sterile, and it is somewhat more difficult to work with than wood—cutting is more tedious.

GLASS, ACRYLIC, AND OTHER PLASTICS

For permanent installation, the greenhouse cover should be glass or acrylic. For a temporary cover, flexible plastic is all right. If you live in a cold climate, you may want to double-glaze the panes of the greenhouse; leave a ½-inch air space between the two pieces of glass or acrylic to cut heat loss approximately 30 percent.

Glass is sold on the even inch at glass shops; have the people at the shop cut the glass to size for you. Wear gloves when handling glass to prevent cuts. Ask for double strength glass of B quality (DSB). This glass, approximately 1/8 inch thick, is fine for most greenhouses. If you want thicker panes ask for 7/32-inch crystal—but remember that the thicker the glass, the heavier the piece. Glaze the glass in wooden sashes with caulking compound (sold at glass stores).

Acrylic is also sold in even inches. If you use four sheets of acrylic for the greenhouse, as is most often done, you can have the sheets cut to size. Acrylic's great advantage is its relatively light weight. Select ¼-inch thick acrylic, and install it as you would glass. Join the sheets at the cut edges with sealant (available at acrylic dealers). The bonding is simple to do, watertight, and permanent. Because window greenhouses are full of plants, obscuring a clear view of the panes themselves, you can economize by buying acrylic seconds. These have some hairline scratches but are much cheaper than first-quality acrylic.

If you want a temporary cover for the window greenhouse—perhaps you do not have enough money at the moment—use any of the flexible plastics that lumber yards carry. Flat rigid plastic can also be used, but you cannot see clearly through it and it is not handsome in the home.

Glass, acrylic, and other plastics have relative advantages and disadvantages. Be aware of these before you select a cover.

SHELVES AND SUPPORTS

Most prefabricated window greenhouses come with glass shelves, but if you make your own greenhouse you must provide shelves and supports yourself. In my acrylic greenhouse I used acrylic bars, which I purchased cut to size from the supplier. I cemented these to the sides and inserted glass shelves. This is an easy installation and works very well.

The support that holds the shelf must be anchored securely to the window greenhouse itself to hold the shelf and the weight

A small commercial plastic window greenhouse; highly durable and weatherable, lightweight and easy to clean. *(Photo courtesy Rohm and Haas).*

of your plants. Haphazard construction will cause accidents with falling plants, so do be careful and really secure the supports in place—whether they are wood, acrylic, or whatever.

The support that holds the shelf must be anchored securely to the window greenhouse itself to hold the shelf and the weight of your plants. Haphazard construction will cause accidents with falling plants, so do be careful and really secure the supports in place—whether they are wood, acrylic, or whatever.

Although glass and acrylic are the accepted shelving materials, waffle-type plastics and preformed rigid plastic devices can also be used; wire shelving, too, is an alternative, but it is rarely esthetically pleasing. If installed properly, wood looks handsome; use redwood strips spaced ½ inch apart on suitable supports.

This type of wooden shelving lets air enter the bottoms of the pots, which is good for the plants; its disadvantage is that it blocks some light. Acrylic and glass let maximum light reach the plants.

In any case, no matter what the material, do not try to span more than 30 inches without installing midsupports—unless you are using acrylic or glass at least ¼ inch thick. Clay pots filled with soil can be very heavy! My window greenhouse is 40 inches in width, and I used ¼-inch crystal glass shelves; each shelf holds twelve 8-inch pots satisfactorily.

HEATING

If the window greenhouse is properly built and there are no air leaks, it should maintain a moderate temperature, even on cold nights. You can regulate temperature and air circulation by opening or closing the window. If you live in a region with very cold winters, you might want to install some weather-stripping; or insert a sheet of flexible plastic about 1 inch from the glass or acrylic to form an air cushion that keeps heat in the greenhouse. Another solution is to use a small space heater (the type used for heating bathrooms); these heaters are sold in department and drug stores. Keep a thermometer inside the greenhouse so you can tell the temperature at a glance. During winter nights try to maintain a minimum temperature of 60°F.

Ventilating the greenhouse is no problem if you have a hinged top and existing window sash to make adjustments. If it gets excessively hot or stuffy in the growing area, try a small fan at low speed.

12 Displaying Greenhouse Plants

In your greenhouse the plants will be grown in containers. But where do the containers go? You cannot just set plants haphazardly on the floor or hang a few here and there. You want your greenhouse to be inviting, and to accomplish this you must properly display all the green accents. What you want is greenhouse furniture: trays, shelves, trellises, planters, and benches, which are all part of the total greenhouse picture. Here we will introduce you to some of the commercially made accessories and also discuss custom-made and do-it-yourself furnishings for growing plants. Note that the commercial benches are bulky, not that attractive, and come in only certain sizes. Building your own benches and shelves will enable you to both save money and create pleasant designs.

BENCHES

A bench is a table with legs, usually of redwood, with a depth of 4 to 6 inches. The space under a bench can be used for potted plants that need shade. However, this arrangement is not attractive, so enclose the bottom with a

Benches in tiers are always convenient for potted plants and look nice too. Benches of this kind make it easy to see and reach all plants, an important part of good greenhouse gardening. *(Photo by Matthew Barr).*

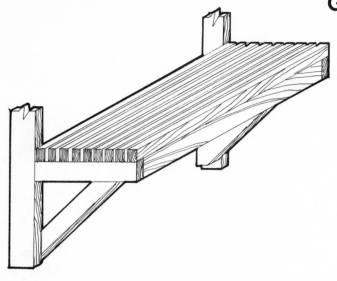

GREENHOUSE FURNISHINGS

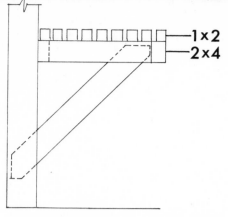

1×2
2×4

NOTE: USE ALL REDWOOD

Potting Tables

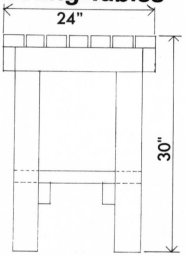

24"

30"

Portable Planter

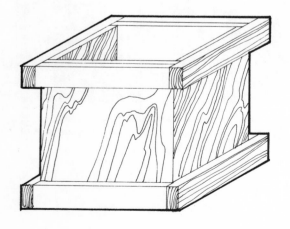

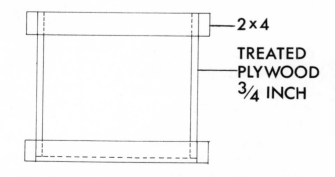

2×4

TREATED PLYWOOD 3/4 INCH

Slatted benches of redwood in this greenhouse are excellent because air is able to reach bottom of plant containers. Also, excess water spill is no problem. *(Photo by Matthew Barr).*

panel of trellage, which lets light and air circulate yet looks good. If you have an A frame greenhouse, put a bench on each side; for a lean-to, use one side for a bench. In the dome greenhouse you can place made-to-fit benches around the perimeter of the "room." Any bench should be waist high, so you can "work" on it. You can fill benches with soil and plant directly into them, put potted plants and flats in trays and then display the plants on the benches, or fill the benches with cinders or gravel and then place potted plants on top of this material. The third choice gives you the flexibility of moving plants around at will—if one arrangement does not suit you, try another.

If you build your own benches, space redwood boards or slats ¼ inch apart to allow for water drainage. Use wooden posts or galvanized pipes from suppliers. To keep soil from shifting through the boards, nail fine-grade mesh hardware cloth underneath the bench. Do not make benches too wide (more than 36 inches) or you will be unable to reach the farthest plants, those against the wall. A width of 6 to 8 inches gives you ample planting space. Greenhouse suppliers sell prefabricated greenhouse benches that you put together, but they are expensive.

Plant pedestals and stands of redwood and of varying heights, from 2 to 4 feet, also provide a handsome setting for plants. Place them in various areas to create an eye-pleasing design.

Not a bench in the strict sense of the word, but equally necessary in the greenhouse is a potting table or workbench, as a place to keep supplies, including soil. Make your own workbench, or buy a commercial one, which will be quite convenient. The workbench, from Christen, Inc., of St. Louis, Missouri, has plastic bins for soil and gravel, a bottom shelf for storing extra pots, and a small sink area. The workbench will take up some of your space, but it will save walking and searching.

Pots can be suspended from ridges to hold plants to use ceiling space, or can also be set on shelves. *(Photo by Pat Matsumoto).*

Trays

As mentioned, you can either plant directly into benches or use trays or pots on them. The definition of a tray is rather confusing: it can be anything from a shallow trough to a box. For our purposes we will consider a tray as a plant box for either starting seeds or cuttings, or for putting potted plants in (the tray then serves as a platform, elevating the plants).

Plastic trays in various sizes will do nicely, or you can make your own from five pieces of redwood. (You decide the size.) Nail together the corners, add a little epoxy at each joint, drill some drainage holes in the bottom, and then attach the bottom.

Shelves

Glass, acrylic, or redwood shelves are frequently overlooked, but they are important items of greenhouse furniture because they allow you to use the interior space to the fullest. For redwood shelves use 6-foot long 2 X 2 slats spaced ¼ inch apart on heavy-duty galvanized L brackets. Five or six slats will give you some space for large pots too. Brace the slats every 3 feet. Mullions in greenhouse windows are narrow, so conventional hardware will not be of any use if you put shelves in windows. However, there is enough wood around the mullions to put some screw eyes into; hang shelves from the eyes

with ropes or chains. This is not the easiest or best shelf design, but it does work. Also use the back or house wall of the A frame or lean-to for shelves. Attach the trays with L brackets (available in many lengths, with the 7-inch the most popular) or similar shelf-supporting devices, like the adjustable Garcy brackets.

If you are having shelves made or are making your own, plan a minimum width of 6 inches—10 is better if space allows. A 6-inch shelf will hold only a few small pots; large containers need a wide shelf. Never span more than 36 inches, and for glass shelves do use substantial 3/16-inch-thick glass for the best support. Always have glass or acrylic edges polished smooth so you will not cut your hands. If you decide to use redwood, again, make the shelves wide enough. Redwood's advantage over glass or acrylic is that it can be easily drilled; its disadvantage is that is blocks out some light.

If you use shelves, do not let the plants' foliage touch the glass because this injures leaves. Have 1 inch of space between the foliage and the glass.

Trellises

Trellises, usually lovely structures used for outdoor growing, are just as lovely indoors and utilize otherwise wasted vertical (wall) space. Vertical growing has been ignored, yet many plants, such as squash, cucumbers, nasturtiums, and morning glories, are natural climbers. Use several trellises in the greenhouse, even if only on one wall.

You can buy ready-made trellises, but they are flimsy and rarely fit the space you have. You can simply and inexpensively make trellises from redwood lath (sold in bundles at lumber houses). The grid pattern, the easiest to build, requires a frame of 2 X 4s. Nail the lath vertically and horizontally on the frame to create a pleasing pattern. Redwood will last many years in the greenhouse without preservative coating, and most plants look good against natural wood.

Planters

Planters are deep (8 inches) rectangular or square boxes in which you grow plants directly in soil. The planter is really a blown-up version of the tray. As with the homemade tray, you can make a planter with five pieces of redwood. Such planters, built to fit the space you have, are extremely handsome and have the custom-made look commercial

planters do not. Window boxes, whether plastic or wood, are essentially planters and are the right depth, but there are many different sizes in terms of length. Before buying a window box from a nursery or greenhouse supplier, measure for the size you want.

Closeup of simple bench construction; redwood is used throughout, treated, and makes a fine building material within a greenhouse. *(Photo by G. Burgess).*

Photo by Clark Photo Graphics

13 Yearly Calendar For Your Greenhouse

If you enjoyed your greenhouse during the summer and spring months, in January you will really realize why greenhouses are so desirable. In this gray, cold month, flowers at the windows are a joy, and a verdant greenery inside while all is bare outside lifts the spirits considerably.

January

But although January is a month of beauty inside, it is also a month to do things in the greenhouse to have spring-flowering plants.

From late January on you can start Hyacinth, Daffodils, Crocus, Grape Hyacinths, and Snowdrops (bulbs). Keep the plants in semi-shade until leaves are at least 4 to 5 inches tall; then bring them into bright light. You can also start caladiums and other tuberous plants and root cuttings of house plants.

Sow some perennial seed so you will have summer bloom. Try cornflowers, clarkias, impatiens, larkspur, marigolds, petunias, snapdragons, statice, and sweet peas, and so on.

Water plants sparsely, especially on dark days; few plants die from not enough water in winter, but overwatering coupled with dark days can cause fungus to attack and kill them. Even though it is cold outside, be sure some fresh air gets into the greenhouse. Open windows slightly in midday; close them at night. Perhaps keep a small electric fan running to keep air circulating. Provide adequate artificial heat to keep temperature at 75F by day, 10 to 15 degrees lower at night. Do not let the house get too warm.

February

It may not look like spring outdoors, but in your greenhouse plants will already be awakening with new sprouts and shoots. This is the time to sow seed and increase watering somewhat and to be prepared for the upcoming sunnier days. Repot some plants (the rest can wait until next month).

Cineraria and Cyclamen should be available as florist plants now, and a few to perk up the greenhouse would be welcome. All kinds of tubers can be started, including Achimenes and Caladiums. Trim houseplants and give them some fresh soil.

Provide adequate ventilation to maintain a healthy atmosphere, and also carefully protect plants against sudden February wind storms. Provide shutters or at least some burlap or some drapery at windows if you feel ambitious.

Seed to sow:
Candytuft
Cyclamen
Kalanchoe
Marigold
Primrose
Snapdragon
Sweet peas
Thunbergia

March

This is a very busy month in the greenhouse. Now is the time to start seeds of annuals and perennials so plants will be ready

Photo by Pat Matsumoto

for outdoors. Make sure the greenhouse has adequate circulation of air: not too cold, not too warm. Watch out for leaf burn on houseplants such as African violets and ferns. Some shade-protection might be necessary if you have an all-glass greenhouse.

Start vegetables for that basket bounty in summer. Get the seeds in or use prestarted plants if they are available. Lettuce can be grown in hanging baskets and root crops started in deep planter boxes or tubs.

Do all kinds of cuttings now if you want to multiply your houseplant stock, and increase your stock of Dalias by dividing bulbs.

With the coming of warm weather insect eggs may start to hatch, so watch plants; if you see insects, eliminate them.

April

April sun can be hot, so shading may now be necessary to protect plants from leaf burn. Be especially prudent about watering plants, and be sure soil is evenly moist. With good weather and warmth plants can use plenty of water. Many annual and perennial seeds and some vegetables can still be started. For tub growing try midget varieties such as eggplant, peppers, cucumbers, and tomatoes. Also grow some radishes and carrots for summer produce. Remember to give vegetables lots of sun and water. Do the rest of the repotting of houseplants and other general chores such as trimming and pruning to prepare for the coming summer months.

Seeds to sow:
  Anemone
  Aster
  Celosia
  Freesia
  Primrose
  Snapdragon
  Zinnia

May

Be sure plants have protection from the sun; ferns, palms, and orchids will all burn in direct sun. Houseplants can be revitalized easily in the good conditions of the greenhouse, and those already there will start rapid growth. Or you can move houseplants into the house because they are in peak health. Increase watering and start a mild feeding program—there is ample light and sun now, so plants need that added boost of food.

Keep the greenhouse some what humid, and continue a regular watering and feeding program for most of your plants. Transfer vegetables outdoors or into large tubs if you want. Start some vines like Clematis and morning glory to add more color to the greenery. Let them climb on walls and windows for a pleasant picture. There is still time to sow seeds of many annuals and perennials.

June

This month the entire greenhouse assumes a lush look because everything is growing, and rapidly. You will want to spend more time with your plants as they thrive. It is a good idea to do some expert house cleaning and get the greenhouse really clean for summer before weather gets too warm. Inspect plants for insects and use appropriate preventatives if necessary.

Start seeds of tomatoes for a fall crop and some snapdragons for winter bloom. Water plants

Photo by Clark Photo Graphics

copiously and tend those vegetables and herbs (this is the peak growing season).

Keep ventilation at an optimum, and settle back (but not for too long) and enjoy some summer color. Keep the greenhouse warm and humid to help plants grow quickly.

July

In July the main consideration is ample water because everything is growing. The sun is hot, the air is dry, and water is a must. Wet down greenhouse walks to increase humidity, which helps combat high temperatures. Keep air circulating in the greenhouse; open vents and windows so there is a soft flow of air. Mist plants with water to keep down heat, and again inspect plants for insects, which can cause trouble at this time. This is the month to start more seeds, such as:

Browalia
Calceolaria
Calendula
Lupine
Migonette
Nemesia
Snapdragon
Stock
Sweet peas (winter flowering)
Wallflower

August

Although this month is hot, it can also bring some cool nights,

so be prepared. Keep ventilation at the optimum, and eliminate any insects you might find. Keep feeding plants, but start tapering off on watering. This is the last time to pinch back such plants as chrysanthemums and carnations. Have the heating system checked to be sure it is in good working order for the fall and winter season.

Seed to start:
Blue lace flower
Browallia
Calceolaria
Calendula
Lupine
Marigold
Nasturtium
Pansy
Primrose
Snapdragon
Statice
Stock
Sweet peas
Thunbergia

September

September usually brings cool nights and clear days, an ideal tonic for plants. The house may need some heat on some nights to provide warmth and to lower high humidity. To get the greenhouse ready for winter, trim and prune plants, and get houseplants in order. Start resting bulbous plants like Glozinias and Caladiums by putting them in their pots (under benches. Discard plants that did not make it during the year. Do a last insecticide spraying to prevent insects and diseases.

Bulbs to start:

Brodiaea
Calla lily
Calochortus
Freesia
Hyacinth
Ixia
Montbretia
Narcissus
Ornithaogalum
Oxalis
Ranunculus
Sparaxis

October

Pretty much follow September's schedule.

November

November is the time to sit back and enjoy the greenhouse; outdoors things may be slowing down and gray days may occasionally dot the months, but in the greenhouse it is still verdant and lovely. Cloudy weather is part of the month, which means you should taper off watering and feeding. Plants do not need any protection now, and what little sun there is will be welcome. Even though cold weather is on the way, be sure to provide adequate air circulation. Heat will probably be needed full time now but not so much that a stagnant, hot atmosphere is created.

Cuttings of various houseplants and flowering bulbs such as amaryllis, crinium, and veltheimia can still be started.

December

This is the season to enjoy your greenhouse, so do as little work as possible. Color should be splendid now (if you have prepared), and poinsettias, crown of thorns, and Christmas cactus will be in full display. Browallias and oxalis can also add to the color festival this month.

Keep most plants somewhat dry, without additional feeding; although it is cold outdoors, be sure to allow some ventilation in the greenhouse. Be on the alert for fungus disease, which can start with cloudy days and cold weather, and if plants show signs of leaf mildew, apply appropriate remedies.

You can take branches of flowering plants like Japanese quince and cherry and forsythia and force them. All they need is warm water to bear their lovely flowers.

Space all plants, walk through the greenery to appreciate nature and the season.

List of Suppliers

Lumber is available from dealers in your area; I-beams, metal framing from building supply yards. All kinds of glass are at your local glass shops, and flexible and rigid plastic are at hardware stores and building supply houses.

Prefabricated greenhouses are available from dozens of manufacturers. These are the ones I have known through the years and have had correspondence with about their products. In addition to greenhouse kits, most of these companies also carry heaters, fans, and greenhouse accessories such as benches, tables and so forth.

Aluminum Greenhouse Inc.
14615 Lorain Avenue
Cleveland, Ohio 44111
Aluminum-and-glass greenhouses; supplies.

Gothic Arch Greenhouses
P.O. Box 1564
Mobile, Alabama 36601
Gothic arch design greenhouses; redwood-and-fiberglas construction. Supplies.

Environmental Dynamics
P.O. Box 996
Sunnymead, California 92388
Fiberglas and steel design; arches. Supplies.

Lord & Burnham
Irvington, N.Y. 10533
One of the largest manufacturers of aluminum-and-glass greenhouses.

Redwood Domes
P.O. Box 666
Aptos, California 95003
Redwood or metal domes of all types. Supplies.

Casaplanta
16219 Cohasset St.
Van Nuys, California 91406
Mini home greenhouses for apartment, office.

W. Atlee Burpee Company
5275 Burpee Building
Warmister, Pennsylvania 18974
The Burpee "English Greenhouse" is priced slightly under $600

Christen, Inc.
59 Branch St.
St. Louis, Missouri 63147
Greenhouse benches and furniture

Enclosures Inc.
80 Main Street
Moreland, Georgia 30259
Units costing several hundred dollars, and up

Gothic Arch Greenhouses
P.O. Box 1564
Mobile, Alabama 36601
Units costing "about $2.50 per square foot"

Grow House Corp.
2335 Burbank
Dallas, Texas 75235
Window greenhouses

J. A. Nearing Co., Inc.
Janco Greenhouses
Box 348
10788 Tucker Street
Department H-3
Beltsville, Maryland 20705
Units start at $450

Peter Reimuller
P.O. Box 2666-A5
Santa Cruz, California 95063
Units priced from $120

Redfern Pre-Fab Greenhouse
Manufacturing Company
3842 Scott's Valley Drive
Santa Cruz, California 95060

Redman Building Products
2550 Walnut Hill Lane
Dallas, Texas 75229
Window Greenhouses

Sturdi-Built Manufacturing Co.
11304 S.W. Boones' Ferry Road
Portland, Oregon 97219

Sunshine Greenhouses
Box 3577
Torrance, California 90510
Units priced from $100

Texas Greenhouse Company, Inc.
2709 St. Louis Avenue
Ft. Worth, Texas 76110

Turner Greenhouses
Route 117
Goldsboro, North Carolina 27530

Vegetable Factory Greenhouses
P.O. Box 2235
Department H-3
Grand Central Station
New York, New York 10017
Units priced from $500

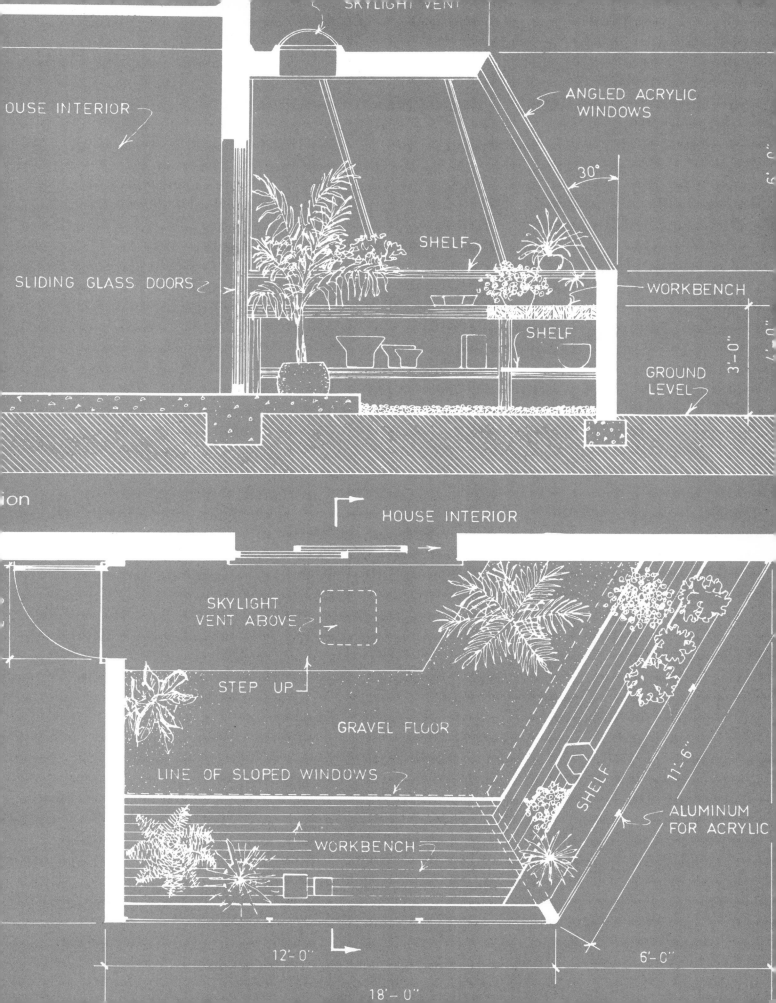

SKYLIGHT VENT

HOUSE INTERIOR

ANGLED ACRYLIC WINDOWS

SLIDING GLASS DOORS

SHELF

30°

WORKBENCH

SHELF

GROUND LEVEL

3'-0"

ion

HOUSE INTERIOR

SKYLIGHT VENT ABOVE

STEP UP

GRAVEL FLOOR

LINE OF SLOPED WINDOWS

SHELF

11'-6"

ALUMINUM FOR ACRYLIC

WORKBENCH

12'-0"

6'-0"

18'-0"